D1597299

Saffron and Pearls

Saffron and Pearls

A memoir of family, friendship & heirloom Hyderabadi recipes

DOREEN HASSAN

Photographs by **Cyrus Dalal**

Edited by **Chinmayee Manjunath**

Harper
Collins

First published in hardback in India by
HarperCollins Publishers in 2018
A-75, Sector 57, Noida, Uttar Pradesh 201301, India
www.harpercollins.co.in

2 4 6 8 10 9 7 5 3 1

Copyright © Doreen Hassan 2018

P-ISBN: 978-93-5277-032-8
E-ISBN: 978-93-5277-033-5

Doreen Hassan asserts the moral right
to be identified as the author of this work.

The views and opinions expressed in this book are the author's own
and the facts are as reported by her,
and the publishers are not in any way liable for the same.
All rights reserved. No part of this publication may be reproduced,
stored in a retrieval system, or transmitted, in any form or by any means,
electronic, mechanical, photocopying, recording or otherwise,
without the prior permission of the publishers.

Designed by Natasha Chandhock

Printed and bound at
Thomson Press (India) Ltd

For my loving husband Peter,
who, true to his name, has always been my rock.
With his love and support, I have been able to
build my world

And my darling children, whom I love very much, and am truly grateful for
Anisha, Vijay, Rhea & Raoul
Nihal, Neha, Anahi & Riaan
Sahil, Neha, Anaia & Aliana

Contents

Foreword

The Hyderabadi believes – '*Khaate waqt aata hai dost. Sotey waqt aata hai dushman.*' (A friend visits at mealtime. An enemy visits while you sleep.) Each culture is known by its culinary traditions, said Abdul Halim Sharar, the prolific Urdu journalist, chronicler and novelist who is best remembered today for his literary publication, *Guzhista Lucknow*. The rare refinement that gave birth to Hyderabadi cuisine can only be understood by reflecting on its history and culture. The roots of what we now know as Hyderabadi cuisine may be traced to a coalescence of several strands of cultural and culinary heritages.

From the foundations of ancient Telangana, the overlapping present states of Maharashtra, Andhra Pradesh, Karnataka and Odisha; and the historical populations from erstwhile Mughal North, Turks, Persians, Arabs, British, not to speak of Kayasthas, Marwaris, Parsis and Bohras – Hyderabadi cuisine as we know it now has all these influences. And as an aside, during British rule, many Lucknowi families, administrators, khansamas, poets and other artists migrated to Hyderabad, which was ruled by the Nizams and known for its extraordinary wealth and opulence. The Awadh dynasty, too, being from the Shia sect had attracted a large number of Persians, or Iranians, and perhaps Peter Hassan's reference to his Iranian roots and its possible influence on his home cuisine in Hyderabad lie there. My own grandmother was a Shia from that region.

The above-mentioned branches and strands of cuisine assimilating an extraordinary range of global diversity in spices, grains, roots, vegetables, fruits, legumes, herbs together with habits and lifestyles of notable order have brought to bear on what is now called Hyderabadi cuisine, which could well be described as Deccani or Dakhni fare or, more appropriately, Nizami cuisine of the state that evolved from the table of the Nizams and the migrant nobility. As there were limited dining options outside, the Hyderabadis entertained mostly at home, hosting elaborate wedding ceremonies and celebrating festivals such as Eid, Ramazan, Diwali and Dussehra.

In the traditional style, old Hyderabadi families ate their daily meals laid out on dastarkhans and they were seated at chowkis during celebrations, festivals and get-togethers. Food was usually served all together but typically eaten in courses. Different communities settled in Hyderabad for long may have some variations in the overall composition of recipes to suit the palate, but broadly the order of service remains the same and individual dishes could be claimed as house specialities indeed as it would be elsewhere. All in all, Hyderabadi cuisine has not been on the sidelines and has an unmistakable imprint on the national stage.

Doreen's wonderful book contains the classic dishes but also several lesser-known recipes. Peter always calls her the anchor of his life, which she is, as she successfully moors the family together and graciously hosts friends, such as myself. For I have been a constant guest at the Hassan home for decades and am truly an example of the fact that khaate waqt aata hai dost! I do believe that this rare cookbook with its priceless recipes and fascinating family history will introduce everyone not just to Hyderabad and its cuisine, but also the Hassan family.

Habib Rehman

*I*ntroduction

A NOTE FROM A FRIEND

When I learnt that Doreen Hassan was working on her food memoir, I was delighted because she is, without a doubt, one of the best cooks and hostesses in the world. She and her husband, Peter Hassan, are not just a lovely couple who are truly made for each other, but are also hosts with the most, as it were! Recently, when Peter found out that I had a day free between the IPL matches in Hyderabad, he flew down from Delhi especially with Doreen and the family and we had one of the most memorable evenings with delicious food and wonderful company. Ours has been a long and cherished friendship.

An invitation to dine at the Hassans' involves not just the finest wines and a spread of food that would make any connoisseur happy, but there is also an eclectic guest list, which encourages scintillating conversation and lively discussions on various topics. One comes back from their home with a full stomach, an engaged, recharged mind and new perspectives. First-time visitors to the Hassans' become friends for life with Peter, Doreen and the rest of the family, of course, but find new acquaintances among their guests too.

While Doreen, whom Peter affectionately calls Doe, always makes sure she welcomes guests and makes them feel at home, she's also in and out of the kitchen, effortlessly ensuring that the meal is done to absolute perfection. I must confess here that I am not a foodie. I've been a frugal eater as I fear putting on weight. I am, therefore, not a good person to invite as the host thinks that I did not enjoy the food. Having said that, when the company is great and the evening enjoyable, then I do let go of my inhibitions and eat to my heart's and stomach's content – maybe seven to ten days a year now. One of these days is invariably at the Hassans' home.

Given their Hyderabadi roots, the biryani that Doreen makes is delicious. The only other one I have eaten that matches up was at Mohammad Azharuddin's home at the start of his Test career; his mother hosted us and all these years later, the flavours still linger in my taste memory. Doreen's biryani is similar and equally memorable; the meat is soft and succulent and the flavour of the rice just makes it divine. There is incredible attention to detail in each dish on the table. In a chicken dish, for example, the meat is sliced into small pieces, and thus doesn't require you to use a knife to cut it, which is ideal when you are pairing it with rice or rotis.

Doreen pays as much attention to the vegetarians among her guests. The Baghare Baingan and Mirchi ka Saalan are always outstanding. I also particularly enjoy the Reshmi Parathas and Sheermals, which are delicately layered and out of this world, especially if you dip them in Hyderabadi Dhal. Most restaurants serve Dal Makhani or Tadka Dal but Hyderabadi Dhal is unique, with just enough spice so it does not overwhelm the other dishes, but enhances them. These are the dishes I remember from all my years of eating Doreen's incredible food, and I am sure this book is a treasure trove of many more recipes.

There is little doubt that everyone who buys this book will add to their culinary expertise and that, I think, is the easy part. What is rarer, and perhaps should be aspired to, is Doreen's unmatched generosity as she watches over her guests. And, finally, her pure joy when they compliment her for the meal she made them. Each and every time.

Sunil Gavaskar

A LIFE OF GOOD FOOD AND WONDERFUL FRIENDSHIPS

*I*f someone were to ask me to describe my life, I would say that I never could stop counting my blessings.

I grew up in a large, loving family and our home in Hyderabad was always open to anyone who wanted to walk in, share a meal, have a laugh and be a friend. And this is still true, decades later, in Delhi – my wife, Doreen, and I share a home with our children, their spouses and grandchildren, and are fortunate enough to have people from all walks of life come home to eat with us and make memories. I firmly believe that generosity and hospitality have very little, or maybe even nothing, to do with money.

When I was growing up, as the eldest of seven children, it was not an extravagant life at all – just a happy one. My mother, Mary Tarachand, was originally from Kolkata but had moved to Hyderabad with her uncle, James Tarachand, who was a very wealthy man, and she was his only ward. I am told by everyone that she was very loved and pampered by her uncle and I remember her as a beautiful person in every respect. I might be biased but she was a legendary beauty and many were supposed to be courting her, fortunately unsuccessfully. My father, Khurshid Hassan, whom everyone – including his children – called Kuchu, was part of a unique and distinguished old Hyderabadi family. His mother, Fakhrul Hajia Begum, was Persian, and his father, Syed Ameer Hassan, was from an aristocratic family with its roots in Etawah, Uttar Pradesh. Several of our family members played a prominent role in India's fight for independence.

Unfortunately, I don't know how my parents met and decided to get married; when I think about it, this match between an aristocratic young woman and a dreamer of a man seems almost like fiction but they were in love. I was born in 1944 in our ancestral home in Lakdi ka Pul, in Hyderabad. My father was a hands-on parent because my mother was often too exhausted to do much but he called her Rani Ma and absolutely doted on her. Every day, he would get all seven of us ready for school, cook the family meals, do everything to keep the house running and manage to keep the atmosphere at home cheerful and hopeful, despite constraints.

Those were magical years for us as a family. Though we faced many challenges, we found comfort and happiness in one another. There was a great emphasis on education and my father made sure we all went to good schools and studied hard. I think the greatest lesson we learnt as children was that love is what is permanent – money comes and goes, luxuries come and go, but if you build strong bonds with family and friends, these become your major asset.

In the first week of every month, we ate well. My father came from a family of food connoisseurs, and he was a brilliant cook. His signature dish was Palak Gosht, which is lamb cooked with spinach. Kuchu would buy the meat from his favourite butcher in Moazzam Jahi Market, and buy ghee from a famous shop called Ahmed Ghee Ghar. At one point, we lived in King Kothi, near the palace; the house had no kitchen and so my father cooked outside, in the open. We children were always fed first and if someone walked into the house as we ate, my father would give them his own plate, with a big smile, and go hungry himself. He was an incredible human being.

Eventually, we moved into a house called Aasra, which means shelter. I had stealthily orchestrated the buying of the house using a signed cheque of my mother's without my parents' permission. Despite that, it all worked out well and Aasra became the first home we owned as a family. In the meantime, I graduated in 1964 and started working, even as I continued my education in a night school. The ₹60 a week that I earned helped run the house.

Tragically, our happy little world was turned upside down on 11 October 1966, when my father passed away from a sudden heart attack. And I found myself the head of the family at twenty-two, with six siblings to look after and prepare respective roadmaps for each.

Forced to find a job that paid well, I travelled to Vishakapatnam to join a company called Coromandel Fertilizers. My cousin, Abid Hussain, who was the collector in that district, had helped me. I reluctantly packed a steel trunk and got on a train to my new life. Initially, I stayed with a friend but my cousin and his lovely wife, Karki, insisted I stay with them, which was incredibly kind and helped keep me sane as I commuted to and from work on a rickety bus, far away from the world I had grown up in. Not only did they give me a roof over my head, but also the abundant love of an adorable couple from

whom I learnt the art of loving and living. I owe an uncountable debt of gratitude to Abid Bhai and Karki Bhabhi for giving me the confidence to live and let live.

Two years later, I came to Hyderabad and started working with Warner Hindustan, which is where I met Doreen, who is a cousin of my dear friend, Eugene Campos. I knew the minute I saw her that I wanted to marry her and we did marry, despite objections. My mother and siblings absolutely doted on Doreen from the minute she first walked into the house, even before we were engaged. We have now been together over forty-five years and I feel grateful that we have built a happy little world full of love and meaningful friendships. Our gratitude remains.

As my father's son and a member of my large-hearted family, hosting people is important to me. If I have time to spare, I like to spend it with people and always say that I would rather make a friend than watch a movie. Doreen has been at the centre of this world – she has supported me, helped me and been a wonderful hostess to everyone who walks into our home. Because you know, when we got married, she did not know how to cook and, above all, she is vegetarian. So, to have learnt all these exquisite dishes from members of our families and recreate them over and over in our home is truly incredible.

Always elegant, inherently beautiful and ever-smiling, she remains our greatest inspiration and this glow has devolved on each member of our immediate family that now numbers a total of fourteen, including me.

Peter Toghrille Hassan

FROM OUR FAMILY TO YOURS

*P*utting this book together, gathering recipes and stories, has really been a journey back in time for me and the family. What made the process of having conversations with family and friends, recounting memories and arguing over anecdotes, gathering photographs and revisiting the past even more special is the fact that in 2016, my husband, Peter (Toghrille to many), and I marked forty-five years of marriage. Like every couple, we've had our ups and downs but, together, Peter and I have managed to make our lives happy and build a world full of love, warmth, friendship and good food. We keep an open house – everyone who steps into our home is always made to feel welcome and is asked to have a meal with us. And this has been important to us because hospitality and generosity are among the many gifts we have inherited from our Hyderabadi lineage.

When we moved to Delhi in 1976 as a young couple with two small children, it was not always possible to host elaborate meals but we did the best we could with what we had. It's funny and emotional for me to think back to that time because I did not even know how to cook! Peter would order in meals, or we would depend on the household staff to help us. And now when I effortlessly draw up menus, get in the kitchen to make elaborate dishes and receive compliments for our table, I often remember the young woman I used to be who didn't even know how to make tea. I still don't make tea, I must confess, but I have managed to carry forward the culinary traditions of both our families, and the city we call home.

I was born in Secunderabad into a Goan Christian family, the Fernes. We trace our lineage back to the Chitrapur Saraswats, a small, Konkani-speaking Brahmin community that shares its genealogy with Kashmiri Pundits. At

the time of the Portuguese rule in Goa, many Saraswats converted to Christianity and my family was one of them. Our roots lie in Saligao, one of the greenest and most quaint villages in Goa, but my father's mother was born and raised in Hyderabad and after marrying her, my grandfather, who had lived in Goa and Uganda, made the city his home too. He joined his father-in-law's chemist business and set up a dispensing chemist shop, called J. Faust & Company in Secunderabad; my father, Lui Fernes, took over the business with my uncle and ran the shop.

My mother Emma's family were from Assagaon, in Bardez, Goa, but she was born and raised in Karachi. In 1948, my parents were married and my mother moved to Faust Mansion, the family home in Secunderabad. I was born in Faust Mansion, which was a traditional Goan home in the middle of a cosmopolitan city. We led a simple life as a large family, and our days were governed by church, work or school, meals and the time spent together. I grew up not eating meat, much like my father, I ate seafood though and still do. The food in our home was traditional Goan cuisine.

My grandmother, Armin, whom I called Mama, was a fabulous cook. She had mastered the best of Goan dishes – prawn curries, fish curries, vindaloo, sorpotel and so much more. She was famous in the community for her feasts at festivals and she even made a range of jams at home, which we would relish at breakfast. We never ate Hyderabadi food; at the most, one of my aunts would make a biryani and raita to take with us whenever we went on a picnic.

I studied at St Ann's Convent, which is still considered one of the best schools in the city. Two of my aunts taught there, so even when I was out of the house, I couldn't get up to any mischief! When I finished college, however, I wanted to start working, to step out of the small little world that had nurtured me, and see what lay outside. Luckily for me, a family friend who worked with a company called Warner Hindustan offered to have me work in the same

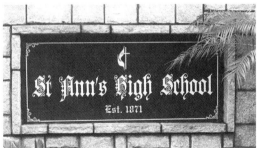

office. My parents agreed and took comfort in the fact that he would pick me up every morning and drop me home every evening. I loved working, and for the first six to eight months, things were quiet in the office because the firm was in the process of moving its factory and administrative operations to Hyderabad. I had no idea how my life was going to change as work in the office began to pick up speed and new people joined the team.

One of them was Peter Toghrille Hassan who was my cousin Eugene Campos's best friend. At the time, Eugene was courting Marie Hyde, another cousin of mine. He'd mentioned that his friend was joining Warner Hindustan and he told this friend that I was also working there. Every day when he would come home to see Marie, Eugene would ask me if his friend Peter had started working with us and I would tell him I had not noticed anyone new but would find out. Finally, one evening, I decided to ask Mr Moses, our personnel manager, if a Peter Hassan had joined and he said no, but there was a young man by the name of Toghrille Hassan who was starting work the next day. The two names did not even sound remotely alike, which confused me.

While I was talking to Mr Moses, the other girls were around and one of them said, 'I saw him when he came for the interview. He is very handsome and I have my eyes set on him, so everyone please stay away.' I rolled my eyes and thought, 'He's all yours, I only asked so that I could finally give Eugene an answer.'

The next day when he came to work and we were introduced to each other as Miss Fernes` and Mr Hassan, he asked me if I was Eugene's cousin and I asked if he was Eugene's friend. I don't know if it was love at first sight, but now when I look back it probably was because that conversation sealed our destinies together. The year was 1968.

I left Warner Hindustan eventually, and started working with the Vazir Sultan Company but Peter and I stayed in touch. This was not easy for me to do because I was not allowed to go out of the house alone, except to work but we managed and spoke a lot over the telephone. By 1970, we were sure we wanted to spend our lives together, but there was the matter of convincing my parents. When Peter came home to ask my parents for my hand in marriage, they were completely against it, but I was prepared to

leave home for him. Seeing that my mind was made up, and watching me walk out of the house convinced my parents to at least consider the idea. They promised me that I could get engaged to Peter but, in return, I had to promise to wait a year to get married.

Eventually, we were married on 19 June 1971. Decades later, we have a home filled with our three children, Anisha, Nihal and Sahil, their lovely spouses – our son-in-law, Vijay, and our daughters-in-law, who are both called Neha; and our six gorgeous grandchildren, Rhea, Raoul, Anaia, Aliana, Anahi and Riaan. We are a family that loves to cook, loves to eat and loves to share our world with everyone we know. The Hassans are a very multi-cultural clan, and our home is the same – we celebrate almost every religious festival because we have family members who are Christian, Muslim, Hindu and Sikh. The tentwallah who comes home to set things up for us once said to me – 'You celebrate everything from Eid to Diwali to Christmas on the same scale. I have never seen a home like this!'

Which is why writing this book is so important for me. All the recipes in it come from members of our family. Because we often host people for meals, I have cooked these recipes countless times over the years, and they have won us precious friendships and priceless memories. The stories pay homage to our families, friends and well-wishers and especially to Hyderabad, the city that we carry in our hearts wherever we go.

I hope that this food will become a part of your life, and your table, too, and that it will bring you the love, warmth and happiness that it has brought generations of our family.

Doreen Hassan

The Hassans of Hyderabad

The heirloom recipes in this book are reflective of Hyderabad's ancient, multicultural history and before I give you more practical tips and pieces of advice on the recipes, I thought it might be interesting to delve into some history – of Hyderabad, and of our family.

What we recognize as Hyderabadi food today owes its origins to the Qutub Shahi dynasty which ruled over the erstwhile kingdom of Golconda for 169 years, from 1518 to 1687 before being conquered by the Mughals. Before the Qutub Shahi era, the region was ruled by the Kakatiya dynasty of Warangal and had also been a part of the Bahmani kingdom, which was based in Bidar that is now part of Karnataka. Sultan Mohammed Quli, a Qutub Shahi king, built Hyderabad in the 1580s, and was inspired by the beautiful, legendary Persian city of Isfahan. Poets, travellers, kings and common men alike sung praises of this new city, which though ruled by devout Shia Muslims, was very secular, multicultural and a haven for arts and literature. The Qutub Shahi rulers were also great connoisseurs of food and their cuisine married Turkish and Persian influences with local ingredients and culinary traditions.

When the Mughals defeated the Qutub Shahi rulers and staked their claim over the kingdom, they chose to move the centre of power from Golconda to Hyderabad and appointed a governor for South India, with the title of Nizam-ul-Mulk. Eventually, the governor's title was changed by the Mughals to Asaf Jah, giving birth to the Asaf Jahi dynasty, which ruled over Hyderabad for two centuries, from 1724 to 1948, when the state was annexed by a newly independent India. The Nizams were, also, discerning gourmets and brought in culinary influences from Telangana, Marathwada and Karnataka.

Our family, the Hassans, have been a part of Hyderabad's history and played a role in India's fight for independence. We have been told by older members of the family that when Peter's father and his siblings were growing up, Hyderabad was a staunchly secular kingdom, embracing the traditions and cultures of all religions. Peter's father, Syed Khurshid Hassan, was one of ten children born to Syed Ameer Hassan, a commissioner in Hyderabad under the Nizam's rule, and his Iranian wife, Fakhrul Hajia Begum, who was from Shiraz. They were one of the first families to boycott British goods and burnt their British-made possessions in a bonfire in front of the family home, Abid Manzil.

At a time when aristocratic families patronized fine fabrics from Europe, the Hassans

favoured Indian textiles. Peter's grandmother, a strident and respected matriarch, was so staunchly anti-British that she sent her sons to Germany for higher education, and was an early supporter of the movement to spin and wear khadi. Three of Peter's uncles – Badrul, Hadi and Abid Hassan – were particularly involved in the Indian independence movement. A close associate of Mahatma Gandhi's, Badrul Hassan owned the first Cottage Industries Emporium in Hyderabad as well as the city's first bookshop, The Hyderabad Book Company.

Hadi Hassan was a botanist and a scholar of Persian literature, while also playing a very important role in the independence movement, winning the admiration of leaders like Gandhi and Sarojini Naidu. He inherited a love of Persian from his Iranian mother and was decorated in 1960 with the Nishan-e-Danish of the First Order, which is Iran's highest academic award. He also established a medical college at Aligarh Muslim University.

Abid Hassan, who was also known as Abid Hassan Safrani, was Netaji Subhash Chandra Bose's personal secretary and interpreter. He took on the role out of admiration for Netaji's revival of the Indian National Army, which had been set up in Japan by a group of Indian prisoners of war led by Captain Mohan Singh during World War II. He chose to add 'Safrani' to his name as a mark of communal harmony and is credited with creating the greeting 'Jai Hind' after Netaji requested him to think of a secular phrase that Indians could use as a mark of national pride.

For a family that was immersed in the politics and public life of the time, the Hassans retained their sense of humour and a great love for food, family and friendships. When I spoke with Peter's cousins, Bizeth and Sanjar in Hyderabad while researching the book, they told me that while the men were illustrious and authoritative outside of the house, at home it was the women who commanded absolute respect.

From them, I have learnt that what makes Hyderabadi food so delicious and unique is the attention paid to every detail and technique, from marinating the meat and grinding masalas to the process of cooking, and then the garnishes, as well as how the dish is served. For example, the secret of a good saalan lies in the grinding of its masala, which must have the texture of silk. The stories of legendary hospitality and rich feasts are far too many to recount, and we have attempted to retain that vibrant spirit of the family through the recipes in this book.

How to Use this Book

BEFORE YOU START

As someone who learnt cooking herself by trial and error, I want to reassure you that while some recipes might appear to be difficult, each recipe can be made by anyone.

In many ways, our home in Delhi is an old-fashioned household when it comes to the way we cook. I prefer adhering to traditional techniques and use traditional cookware too. However, I am aware that modern kitchens might not be equipped for this, so if you do not own a lagan, and are not keen to buy one, please use a grill pan or any pan of your choice. You can improvise as required. My advice to you would be to read a recipe very carefully before you attempt it, so that you know what to prepare for in advance. For example, marinating meat well ahead of time or grinding certain masalas before you start cooking. The more complex dishes might need some practice and I have indicated that in my notes where relevant.

The chapters are arranged to echo my own culinary journey. Each chapter begins with the easiest dish and progresses to more difficult ones. My hope is for you to make these dishes your own, tweaking an ingredient or technique to suit your tastes, and sharing them with friends and family. This would make me the happiest.

THE ESSENTIALS

TRADITIONAL UTENSILS

The main utensils used for cooking Hyderabadi dishes are the degchi, kadhai, deg, lagan, tawa and a good frying pan. You may already own most of these utensils.

Degchi – A thick, round-bottomed, wide-necked cooking pot with a well-fitting lid, it is generally used for slow cooking of dishes with a lot of gravy.

Kadhai – Like the Chinese wok, this utensil is also thick and heavy-bottomed but it has a loose-fitting lid. We use it for deep frying or cooking meats and vegetables.

Tawa – A flat, thick iron alloy griddle mainly used for the preparation of rotis and parathas.

Lagan – A wide, round, heavy-bottomed utensil made of copper and tin-plated on the inside. A lagan is about 2½" in height.

Frying pan – These come in many sizes, but I recommend investing in a small, round, 1"-high pan with a long handle. You can use it to fry and roast masalas, and to do the baghaar for dishes.

MEASURES AND CONVERSIONS

Dry weight measures, as used in this book

200 gm rice	-	1 cup
200 gm sugar	-	1 cup
100 gm flour	-	1 cup
100 gm butter	-	1/2 cup

Liquid measures, as used in this book

250 ml	-	1 cup
125 ml	-	1/2 cup
15 ml	-	1 tablespoon
7.5 ml	-	1/2 tablespoon
5 ml	-	1 teaspoon
2.5 ml	-	1/2 teaspoon
1.25 ml	-	1/4 teaspoon

Estimations

One kilogram rice for twelve to fifteen people
One kilogram lentils for about twenty people
One kilogram mutton for eight to ten people
One kilogram vegetables for six to eight people
One kilogram chicken for six to eight people
One kilogram fish for eight to ten people
One kilogram prawns for ten to twelve people

Kitchen Wisdom

GINGER-GARLIC PASTE

It's very simple to make and keeps well in the fridge for a month at least if you store it at the back of a shelf. The ratio I use is a kilogram of ginger to 750 gm of garlic. Peel both the ginger and garlic and grind to a fine paste using as little water as possible. If you use a grinding stone, you will not need to use any water at all but for convenience and speed, it might be better to use a blender.

PAPAYA PASTE

This is used to tenderize meat and for one kilogram of mutton, you will need two level teaspoons of papaya paste. You can make this by grinding a medium-sized slice of unpeeled raw papaya to a fine paste in the blender. Measure it out and grind more, if required.

GARAM MASALA POWDER

Every Indian household has their own recipe for garam masala and this is mine. Measure out equal quantities of cardamom, cinnamon sticks and cloves. Grind each one separately into a fine powder. Mix all three together and store in an airtight jar. Make sure you use it before the fragrance fades.

TAMARIND PURÉE

Soak a walnut-size ball of tamarind in a cup of warm water for 15 minutes. Squeeze the pulp out and strain.

COCONUT MILK

Grate a fresh coconut. In a bowl, cover the grated flesh with hot water. After a few minutes, using your hands or a muslin cloth, squeeze out the juice into a separate bowl. This is known as the thick milk or first extraction. Add in another cup of hot water and squeeze out the remaining juice. This is the thin milk or second extraction. In a recipe, you will always add the thin milk first. The thick milk is blended into a dish at the very end, to add creaminess and flavour.

HOW TO SET YOGURT

I recommend you purchase an earthenware bowl for this purpose and the yogurt will have an addictive, unique flavour. Boil milk and cool till it is lukewarm. Rub a spoonful of leftover yogurt and all over the insides of an earthenware bowl. Pour the warm milk into the bowl, cover and keep in a warm place to set. If you want sour yogurt, use yogurt which is two days old.

HOW TO MAKE HARD BOILED EGGS

Boil water in a deep saucepan or vessel and carefully add the eggs in. The water should be high enough to cover the eggs. Boil for 8 to 9 minutes. Take the eggs out using a spatula and crack the shell gently. Immerse the eggs immediately in cold water for a few minutes until they get cool enough to handle. You can peel the shell off very easily.

NOTES ON BUYING AND COOKING MUTTON

Mutton is every Hyderabadi's favourite meat. The day would traditionally begin with Nehari, which is a soup cooked overnight with lamb trotters and tongue, and eaten with kulchas. Other popular breakfast dishes are Kheema and parathas, and Kaleji Gurda. When you are cooking with mutton, the quality of the meat is very important. I have a butcher that I can rely on but still prefer to go buy the mutton myself, choosing the calf of the leg or shin bone (called Adla Kareli or Machli ka Gosht). Pasinda meat, which is specified in many recipes, is a steak cut with marrow bones.

I am told that my father-in-law used to believe that the two people to be carefully watched are the butcher and the goldsmith. If you cannot go buy the meat yourself, please make sure that you send out for or order in from a reliable source.

Mutton must always be cooked at room temperature. So, if you have stored the meat in the fridge or freezer, make sure you thaw it well in advance. It is also best cooked on a slow flame.

HOW TO CLEAN PAYA OR LAMB'S TROTTERS

You must ask your butcher to clean the trotters very well before you buy them. Sometimes, though you might find pieces of skin or strands of hair still on the meat. If you do, please scorch the meat over a flame for a quick minute or scald it for a few minutes in boiling water. Once the meat is clean, rub the trotters with a little gram flour to clean them and then wash thoroughly.

NOTES ON BUYING AND COOKING CHICKEN

Chicken is a healthier meat to choose and earlier, it used to be more expensive than mutton. For a healthy dish, choose to have the skin of the chicken removed, which makes sure there is no fat left in the meat. It has a subtler flavour than mutton, so it is important to flavour a chicken dish with a light hand or the masalas will overpower the meat.

WHAT IS BAGHAR AND HOW IT'S TO BE DONE

Across India, the final seasoning has different names and in Hyderabad, we call it the baghar. It adds flavour and flourish to the dish, and must never be skipped.

The baghar is either done right at the start of cooking (as in Mirchi Ka Saalan, Baghare Baingan and Tamatar ki Chutney) or at the end, when the dish is ready, as with most dhals. Be careful never to add water when doing your baghar. If the baghar is to be done first, ensure that the pan or dish you are cooking in is wiped clean. For the baghar at the end, you might need to purchase a small handheld pan, which you can find at any good store.

I have specified the ingredients for baghar in every recipe, as per the dish. The standard ingredients are dried red chillies, cumin seeds or mustard seeds, garlic cloves and curry leaves. You must heat oil or ghee, or a mixture of both until smoking, and add the ingredients in quickly. Let them splutter and then either add in the other ingredients or pour the baghar over the finished dish. When you do the baghar at the end, make sure you cover the dish as soon as you pour it in. This helps preserve the aroma and the flavours.

COOKING ON DHUM

There are two dhum techniques used in Hyderabadi cooking:

Dhum dena – This means keeping the dish to cook on a slow fire for anything for a few minutes. Traditionally, such dishes are cooked in a wide, shallow pan called a lagan, which is placed on a wood fire, or charcoal fire. This technique makes the oil rise to the surface giving the top layer of the meat or rice a wonderful brown colour. When rice is cooked on dhum in this way, each grain is separate. Where this is required, I have indicated it in the recipe.

Dhum pe pakana – This means cooking the dish on a slow fire. The lagan is covered and slow-burning pieces of charcoal are placed above and below.

so
so
250
25
Lim
Koth
S

and cook the dhal until tender —
and keep aside.
onions and fry in a separate degchi
the onions and keep aside.
see garlic paste and all the
Add curd and fry well —
cooked dhal and mix
d garam masala,
pped hara masala

cook the rice s/y and
ayee of dhal, one 1/a
ons some men —
some
S qus. each

Vegetables
and Dhals

'YOU BETTER LEARN TO COOK'

When Peter and I got engaged, my grandmother, Mama, said to me – 'His family are very good cooks. You better learn to cook or he will get fed up of you soon.'

Mama was an excellent cook but I never learnt from her – I did not think it would matter or that Peter would tire of me if I did not cook! Once we got married, food suddenly became an issue. There was never anything vegetarian on the table and for every meal, Peter used to get idlis, or vadas or a dosa or upma for me from Taj Mahal Hotel, which was close to their house. I would visit my parents and bring back my meals and my mother-in-law, who never cooked herself, liked to taste the food. '*Kya layi*, ma?' she would ask and try a bit of everything. Eventually, she began to get a dhal or sabzi or a tomato chutney made for me at every meal, and it was also my introduction to Hyderabadi food. No one forced me to cook, and I would go into the kitchen only to bake a cake whenever there was a birthday.

Peter and I lived in the family home for three years, during which time we had Anisha, our daughter. When we moved out, it was because we needed more space, and

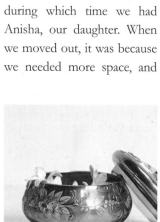

soon Nihal was born. Peter wanted us to live close to either one of our families, and we found a house near my parents' home, which was convenient for me. I had a lady live with us at home to look after the children and she was also a good cook. I was still working at Vazir Sultan and had two little children, so learning to cook was not a priority.

Whenever we had people over, I used to ask my parents to send food across. There was one evening that I still remember and laugh over. A friend of Peter's had sent us a whole lot of prawns from Vizag and we were hosting a dinner that night. Peter asked the chef at a local restaurant, Nanking, if he could help us by cooking the prawns. He did, and prepared a mouth-watering dish of garlic prawns. One of our guests loved it so much that she asked Peter who had made it. Without giving it much thought, he said that I had. And she spent the rest of the evening asking me for the recipe. I literally ran from room to room, trying to avoid her but

she followed me everywhere and it was the funniest dinner party, with a guest chasing the hostess all evening. Eventually I managed to escape the situation.

In 1976, Peter was offered a job with Voltas in Delhi and, after much thought, we decided to move because it held the promise of a better life. It was not an easy step to take – we had our families and friends around us in Hyderabad and it was a very lovely life. But we were also lucky that we could rent a nice house in Defence Colony in Block C and now we live in Block D, so it feels like coming full circle. Back then, Peter moved two or three months ahead of me and I came to Delhi in November.

That first winter was difficult – we had to get used to a new life in a new city. I had brought a couple with me from Hyderabad who worked with us. The husband helped with the housework and the wife cooked but they could not manage in Delhi – I suppose it was too much of a change for them and we had to send them back home. So, I had to do all the housework, along with looking after Anisha and Nihal. It was a very busy time for me. We began to order in food from restaurants and family members kept visiting us over Christmas and the New Year, so we managed somehow but I began to feel that I must really learn to cook now. Ordering in all our meals was not healthy and it was expensive for a young family just starting out.

So early the next year, the children and I went back to Hyderabad with my mother-in-law and a sister-in-law who had been staying with us. Before I left, I promised Peter – 'Either I will learn to cook, or I will find us a good cook.' As it turned out, I just loved being back home and did neither! Finally, Peter called me and said, 'Come back, I have found us a good cook here and he is hard of hearing so no-one will poach him from us.'

I felt so guilty about having done nothing yet that I went to see his aunt, Zehra Alambardar, whom we called Phuppu Jani, and said, 'Please teach me how to make a few dishes.' She was very sweet and told me that she cooked by andaaz, or instinct – 'Beta, I cannot tell you a recipe with measurements. You have to watch and learn. I will make the dishes in front of you, and you write each recipe down, step by step.'

As she measured ingredients out by andaaz, I used spoons to estimate how much she'd used, and she patiently guided me through, step by step, until I learnt how to make Tas Kabab, a mutton biryani, a chicken dish, a simple dhal and Puran Poli. Tas Kabab is still one of Peter's favourites and it's still on the menu for every dinner we host, though my children are tired of it.

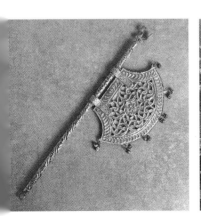

AHI KI KADHI

INGREDIENTS

For the kadhi

11/4 kg thick yogurt

1 cup gram flour

2 large, ripe red tomatoes, roughly chopped

4 sprigs curry leaves

1½ tablespoons coriander powder

1 tablespoon ginger-garlic paste

2 teaspoons red chilli powder

½ teaspoon turmeric powder

A medium bunch coriander leaves

Salt to taste

For the pakoras

1 cup gram flour

2 onions, finely chopped

4 green chillies, finely chopped

2 sprigs coriander leaves, finely chopped

Oil for deep frying

Enough yogurt to form a paste

Length of clean white muslin cloth, to strain

For the baghar

½ cup oil

6 dry red chillies

4 flakes garlic

3 sprigs curry leaves

2 teaspoons cumin seeds

METHOD

TO MAKE THE KADHI

Mix in the yogurt, ginger-garlic paste, chilli powder, salt, coriander powder and gram flour in a large bowl,. Pulp the tomatoes in a blender and add to this mixture. Mix very well.

Drape the muslin cloth over the mouth of a large earthen pot, and strain the yogurt mixture. It might be quite thick, so if you need to use a little water to strain it, please do. The sieved liquid needs to be smooth. Place the earthen pot on a high flame and stir in curry leaves and coriander leaves. Bring the kadhi to a boil and allow to cook until it thickens. Keep stirring it to prevent the gram flour from sticking to the bottom of the pot.

Taste to check if the gram flour's raw flavour has gone, which is when it is done. Take the pot off the flame and allow to cool.

FOR THE PAKORAS

Mix onions, coriander leaves and green chillies with the gram flour and yogurt into a thick batter. Heat oil in a kadhai. When it is hot enough, put in tablespoons of the mixture to form pakoras. Fry until these turn a deep golden brown and remove onto a plate lined with absorbent paper. You can add these pakoras to the kadhi an hour before you serve. Do not add them too early or they will get soggy.

BEFORE YOU SERVE

Heat oil in a small frying pan, until it is smoking. First, toss in the red chillies and garlic; let these turn dark brown and then add in cumin seeds and curry leaves. This baghar needs to be nearly charred for the flavours to deepen. When it is, pour it over the kadhi and cover the pot immediately to prevent the aromas from escaping. Serve at once.

TAMATAR KA KUT

INGREDIENTS

5 kg red tomatoes, cut into quarters

5 eggs, hard boiled and shelled

1 bunch curry leaves

10 tablespoons sesame seeds

5 heaped tablespoons gram flour

5 tablespoons coriander seeds

3 tablespoons red chilli powder

3 tablespoons cumin seeds

2 tablespoons ginger-garlic paste

2 tablespoons fresh heavy cream

Salt to taste

For the baghar

½ cup oil

10 dry red chillies

8 flakes garlic

2 sprigs curry leaves

1 teaspoon cumin seeds

METHOD

Pulse the gram flour in a blender and pass through a sieve to ensure there are no lumps. On a dry tawa or any other flat pan, roast sesame seeds, coriander seeds and cumin seeds. Grind to a fine paste, using a little water. Set aside.

Place the tomato quarters in a large pan, and mix in the red chilli powder, powdered seeds, ginger-garlic paste and curry leaves. Do not add any water – the tomatoes will release enough gravy. Cook on a medium flame, stirring at intervals, until the tomatoes break down and melt. All the ingredients should have blended well together and resemble a thin soup or gravy. Once this is done, take the pan off the flame and let the gravy cool.

Drape a length of clean white muslin over the mouth of another pan, of the same size, and strain the gravy through. Add the powdered gram flour to it and return to the flame; cook until the consistency is that of a thick soup.

FOR THE BAGHAR

Heat oil in a small frying pan, until it is smoking. Toss in red chillies and garlic. When these turn dark brown, add cumin seeds and curry leaves. Fry until nearly charred. Take off the flame and pour into the tomato gravy and cover immediately.

TO SERVE

Decant the gravy into a deep dish. Halve the hard boiled eggs, and garnish the gravy with these. Swirl the cream over and serve immediately.

$\mathcal{T}$AMATAR METHI

INGREDIENTS

½ kg tomatoes, finely chopped

¼ kg green peas, shelled

4 bunches fenugreek leaves

2 onions, finely sliced

2 sprigs curry leaves

4 tablespoons oil

2 teaspoons red chilli powder

1 teaspoon ginger-garlic paste

½ teaspoon cumin seeds

¼ teaspoon turmeric powder

METHOD

Heat oil well in a pan and toss in cumin seeds and curry leaves. When these splutter, add sliced onions and sauté until golden brown. Add ginger-garlic paste and turmeric and chilli powders. Sprinkling in some water, let fry until the raw aromas disappear. Put in the tomatoes and cook until these break down – do not add any water.

Add green peas and cook for about 5 minutes before mixing in the fenugreek leaves. Lower the flame and let cook until the oil rises to the surface and there is no gravy in the pan.

$\mathcal{T}$AMATAR BHINDI

INGREDIENTS

1 kg bhindi

3 onions, sliced length-wise

3 tomatoes

¼ cup oil

2 teaspoons chilli powder

1 teaspoon dried mango powder

1 teaspoon coriander powder

½ teaspoon turmeric powder

Salt to taste

METHOD

Wash and clean the bhindi, and cut into 1" pieces. Chop the tomatoes fine. Heat oil in a pan or kadhai and sauté the onions until they soften.

Add in the bhindi, tomatoes and all the masalas. Lower the heat and cook covered, on dhum, until the bhindi is done.

Tamatar Bhindi

BAGHARE BAINGAN

This is a truly iconic Hyderabadi dish and I am requested to make it more often than I can count. If I know that the people I am serving it to can tolerate the heat, I add more green chillies, which brings out the flavours.

INGREDIENTS

1 kg small, round eggplants
¼ kg onions, finely sliced
1½ cups oil
10 green chillies
4 sprigs curry leaves
4 tablespoons sesame seeds
4 tablespoons ginger-garlic paste
3 tablespoons peanuts
3 tablespoons coriander powder
2 tablespoons cumin seeds

½ teaspoon fenugreek seeds
½ teaspoon onion seeds
½ teaspoon red chilli powder
Pulp from a fistful of tamarind
Salt to taste

For the baghar
1 sprig curry leaves
1 teaspoon cumin seeds
½ teaspoon onion seeds
½ teaspoon fenugreek seeds

METHOD

Roast the coriander powder, peanuts and fenugreek, onion, cumin and sesame seeds together. Grind to a fine paste. Heat oil in a pan, and fry the sliced onions until very brown but not burnt. Or, you can roast the onions, one at a time, directly on the flame. Let each char, and then peel. Grind the fried or charred onions to a fine paste.

Slit each eggplant into four quarters, leaving the stem on. Keep a deep bowl of salted, room-temperature water on hand, and drop each eggplant quarter into it as you slit it. Heat oil in a thick-bottomed, large pan. Add curry leaves, cumin, fenugreek and onion seeds. When these splutter, add the masala paste you ground earlier.

Sauté until it is fragrant and well-browned. Now, add the eggplants and green chillies; cover and let cook on a low flame until almost soft. Pour in tamarind pulp and cook on a medium flame for another 10 minutes or until the gravy is thick. Sprinkle in the coriander leaves and keep on dhum for a few minutes until the oil rises to the surface. You can choose to drain this oil off before you serve the dish.

If you are planning on serving this dish at a dinner, I highly recommend that you make it a day before. Do not refrigerate that night. Leave it out – this allows the flavours to break down and meld together, making the dish much more layered and flavourful. Any leftovers will need to be refrigerated.

MIRCHI KA SAALAN

INGREDIENTS

½ kg fat green chillies, deseeded and de-stemmed

1 dried coconut, grated

1 cup oil

4 onions, lightly fried and ground

8 tablespoons peanuts

4 tablespoons sesame seeds

4 tablespoons coriander seeds

2 tablespoons fenugreek seeds

4 teaspoons cumin seeds

2 teaspoons chilli powder

2 teaspoons ginger-garlic paste

1 teaspoon mustard seeds

½ teaspoon turmeric powder

Pulp from a fistful of tamarind

Salt to taste

For the baghar

2 sprigs curry leaves

1 teaspoon cumin seeds

METHOD

Heat oil in a pan until it is really hot. Add cumin seeds and curry leaves. As soon as these splutter, add green chillies and all the other ingredients, except for the tamarind pulp.

Cook on a low flame until the chillies soften. Do not add in water. Just as the chillies are done, pour in the tamarind pulp and bring to a final boil before taking off the flame.

SAFED MIRCHI KA SAALAN

INGREDIENTS

200 gm fat green chillies, deseeded and de-stemmed

½ cup oil

To be ground together

2 fresh coconuts, grated and finely ground

10 cashew nuts

2 tablespoons chironjee

2 tablespoons poppy seeds

2 tablespoons fenugreek seeds

2 tablespoons cumin seeds

2 tablespoons Bengal gram

Baghar ingredients

2 sprigs curry leaves

1 teaspoon cumin seeds

Juice of 5 lemons

Salt to taste

METHOD

Heat the oil and fry chillies in a pan until they blister. Remove onto a plate lined with absorbent paper and set aside.

Add cumin seeds and curry leaves to the same oil. When these splutter, add the ground masala and sauté until fragrant. Then add in the chillies and cook on a low flame until they soften. Finally, add the lemon juice and bring to a boil before taking the pan off the flame.

Mirchi ka Saalan

CHUKANDAR KI SABJI

INGREDIENTS

4 beetroots, boiled
6 whole red chillies
6 sprigs curry leaves
¼ cup oil

2 tablespoons dried mango powder
1 teaspoon mustard seeds
Salt to taste

METHOD

Peel and cube the beetroots, and set aside.

Heat oil in a pan or kadhai and toss in the red chillies. When these start to darken, add the mustard seeds and curry leaves. Let these splutter, and mix in the beetroot cubes.

Add the dried mango powder and salt a minute or two later, and mix well. Leave the pan on the flame for a few more minutes to let the flavours amalgamate. Once the dish is fragrant, it is done.

KARELA SABJI

INGREDIENTS

½ kg karela, cleaned and sliced
¼ kg onions, sliced
1 small bunch coriander leaves
2 green chillies
2 cups oil, for deep frying
3 tablespoons dried mango powder

½ teaspoon turmeric powder
To be ground into a powder
2 tablespoons coriander seeds
2 tablespoons fennel seeds
1 teaspoon onion seeds

METHOD

Heat the oil in a thick-bottomed pan or kadhai till it just starts to smoke. Deep fry the karela slices until they soften – do not let them turn crisp. Place the fried pieces on plates lined with absorbent paper and set aside.

Heat two tablespoons of oil in a different pan, and sauté the onion slices until they soften. Add chilli and turmeric powders, the ground masala and salt. Mix well and let it cook until fragrant.

Add the karela slices, and cook on a low flame for five to seven minutes. Garnish with the green chillies and coriander leaves before you serve.

Karela Sabji

LOO KHORMA

Very rich and delicious, this can be made only with potatoes, or you can add in eggs. I have given both options in the recipe below.

INGREDIENTS

½ kg potatoes
(if you want to use eggs,
use ¼ kg potatoes and 8 hard boiled eggs)
¼ kg green peas, shelled
1 cup yogurt
2 medium onions, finely sliced
2 green chillies, slit
4 sprigs coriander leaves, chopped
1 sprig mint leaves, chopped

4 tablespoons coconut powder
2 teaspoons poppy seeds
1 teaspoon coriander powder
1 teaspoon ginger-garlic paste
1 teaspoon red chilli powder
1 teaspoon garam masala powder
¼ teaspoon turmeric powder
Salt to taste

METHOD

Peel the potatoes, cut into long slices and soak in a bowl of salted water. If you are using eggs, shell them, cut each into half and keep aside.

Roast and grind the poppy seeds, coconut powder and coriander powder lightly. Heat oil in a pan and fry onions until they turn golden brown. Remove onto a plate lined with absorbent paper, and set aside. Then, grind the fried onions to a paste using a little water. Set aside.

Put the pan back on the stove and heat two teaspoons of oil. Add ginger-garlic paste and chilli and turmeric powders. Sprinkling in a little water to prevent the powders from sticking, sauté for a few minutes. Now, add the roasted masala you prepared earlier and sauté well.

Add the yogurt and cook the gravy until it darkens. Now, add potatoes and three cups of water; let the potatoes soften and when they do, tip in the green peas. Cook for 5 minutes more and add the coriander and mint leaves, garam masala powder and the ground onions. Leave on dhum for 5 minutes and decant into a deep bowl, to contain all the gravy. If you are using eggs, add them to the gravy just before you are ready to eat.

SOOKHI MOONG DHAL

INGREDIENTS

150 gm moong dhal
600 ml water
2 teaspoons ginger-garlic paste
½ teaspoon cumin seeds
½ teaspoon coriander seeds
½ teaspoon chilli powder

Salt to taste
For the baghar
100 gm ghee
5 dry red chillies
1 teaspoon cumin seeds

METHOD

Clean the dhal, wash and drain. In a pan, mix the dhal, all the spices and water; cook on a medium flame until the lentils are soft but not mushy. Mix in the salt and take off the stove.

Heat the ghee in a frying pan, and fry dry red chillies and cumin seeds until these splutter. Pour this baghar over the dhal and mix well.

PALAK AUR CHANA KI DHAL

INGREDIENTS

½ kg spinach leaves, or any
other greens of your choice
100 gm chana dhal
4 dried red chillies
2 green chillies
6 tablespoons oil
2 tablespoons lemon juice

1 teaspoon ginger paste
1 teaspoon coriander seeds
1 teaspoon cumin seeds
1 teaspoon chilli powder
½ teaspoon onion seeds
½ teaspoon mustard seeds
Salt to taste

METHOD

Soak the chana dhal overnight, or for three hours in warm water. Boil on a low flame for 30 minutes in half a litre of water. Wash the greens and drain well; chop and set aside.

Heat oil in a pan and fry onion seeds, mustard seeds and dried red chillies. When these begin to splutter, add spinach and ginger paste, coriander seeds, cumin seeds, chilli powder and salt. Cook on a low heat for about 10 minutes.

Add the chana dhal and mix gently with the spinach. Cook for 5-7 minutes. Add green chillies and squeeze the lemon juice over. Serve as a side to a tomato-based gravy.

*K*HATTI DHAL

Whenever a Hyderabadi craves dhal, it is this version of it. Khatti Dhal is a staple for us and I hope it becomes one of your favourites too.

INGREDIENTS

1 cup masoor dhal

1 cup tuvar dhal

¾ cup tamarind paste

2 tomatoes, roughly chopped

2 slit green chillies

2 sprigs coriander leaves

1 sprig curry leaves

1 tablespoon ginger-garlic paste

1 tablespoon red chilli powder

1 teaspoon turmeric powder

For the baghar

½ cup oil

6 full red chillies

6 garlic cloves

1 sprig curry leaves

2 tablespoons ghee

METHOD

Clean and wash the dhals and soak together for 30 minutes. In a pressure cooker, cook the dhals with ginger-garlic paste, turmeric powder, tomatoes, chilli powder, curry leaves and three cups of water until soft.

Take the cooker off the flame; let it cool off before you open it. Mash the cooked dhal to a fine paste. Add tamarind, slit green chillies, coriander leaves and salt. Return to the stove and cook on a slow fire until the tamarind breaks down, which usually takes 10-15 minutes.

FOR THE BAGHAR

Heat the oil in a small frying pan and then add ghee. When this mixture is smoking hot, add red chillies, garlic and curry leaves. Let these fry until nearly charred. Turn off the flame and quickly pour the baghar over the dhal and close the lid for a few minutes until the spluttering stops. Serve hot.

MITHI DHAL

INGREDIENTS

2 cups water
1 cup moong dhal
3 green chillies
½ bunch coriander leaves
2 teaspoons salt
1 teaspoon ginger-garlic paste
1 teaspoon oil

For the baghar
4 dry red chillies
1 sprig curry leaves
2 tablespoons oil
1 tablespoon ghee
1 teaspoon cumin seeds

METHOD

Boil the dhal and all the other ingredients until the water dries up and the dhal is soft. Then, take it off the flame and mash the dhal into a paste. Now, add three cups of water – more, if you like your dhal to be thinner – and bring it back to the boil. Lower the flame and simmer for 10-15 minutes.

FOR THE BAGHAR

Heat oil and ghee in a small frying pan until smoking. Toss in red chillies, curry leaves, and cumin seeds. Allow these to brown until they are nearly charred, and pour the baghar into the dhal. Cover the pan immediately. If you want a more indulgent dish, swirl a tablespoon of fresh cream into the dhal before you serve it.

MASH KI DHAL

INGREDIENTS

600 ml water
100 gm urad dhal
2 garlic cloves, peeled and chopped
2 green chillies, chopped

1 small onion, finely sliced
2 tablespoons ghee
1 teaspoon ginger paste
Salt to taste

METHOD

Wash urad dhal in a pan; add water and ginger paste. Bring it to a boil and simmer until the dhal is cooked and the water has evaporated. Take off the stove and mix in the salt. In a small frying pan, heat ghee and sauté onion until golden brown.

Toss in the chopped garlic and green chillies for just a minute and pour this baghar onto the dhal. Mix well, garnish with mint leaves and serve.

Mash Ki Dhal

KHADI DHAL

INGREDIENTS

300 ml water

100 gm masoor dhal

1 small bunch coriander leaves, finely chopped

1 small bunch spring onions,
or 1 onion, finely chopped

1 green chilli, chopped

6 tablespoons oil

2 teaspoons ginger-garlic paste

½ teaspoon turmeric powder

Salt to taste

METHOD

Wash the dhal and soak in water for about 30 minutes. In a pan, heat oil and sauté spring onions/onions until quite browned. Lower the heat, and add ginger-garlic paste and turmeric. Sauté to let the flavours blend. Add the dhal, along with the water it was soaking in.

Cook until the dhal is soft, and then mix in salt. Take off the flame and decant into a serving dish. Garnish with chopped green chillies and, if you wish, finely chopped coriander leaves.

KADDU KA DALCHA

INGREDIENTS

1 large pumpkin, cubed

½ kg tomatoes, chopped

¼ kg split gram lentils

100 gm tamarind, pulped

4 green chillies, slit

1 onion, finely sliced

2 bunches coriander leaves, finely chopped

3 cinnamon sticks, powdered

3 tablespoons oil

1½ teaspoons ginger-garlic paste

1 teaspoon red chilli powder

½ teaspoon turmeric powder

Salt to taste

METHOD

Pressure cook the lentils, mash to a fine paste and set aside. In a pan, heat oil and fry the onion until it turns golden brown. Add ginger-garlic paste and chilli powder. Sprinkle water at intervals and sauté the masalas until fragrant. Add in the pumpkin cubes. Then, add the tomatoes and cook until the pumpkin cubes are soft.

Pour in the mashed dhal and add curry leaves, cinnamon powder and green chillies. Mix well and add tamarind juice. Bring to the boil and sprinkle with the coriander leaves. Keep on dhum for 5 minutes before taking it off the flame.

Kaddu ka Dalcha

NARANGI DHAL

This family recipe is very unusual and delicious. The oranges add immense flavour. We use Indian oranges or narangis.

INGREDIENTS

1 cup moong dhal

3 tomatoes, chopped

2 oranges

2 green chillies, slit

2 sprigs coriander leaves, finely chopped

1 sprig curry leaves

1 tablespoon ginger-garlic paste

1 tablespoon chilli powder

Salt to taste

For the baghar

½ cup oil

6 whole red chillies

6 garlic cloves

1 sprig curry leaves

2 tablespoons ghee

1 teaspoon cumin seeds

METHOD

Clean and wash the dhal, and leave it to soak for 30 minutes. In a pressure cooker, cook the dhal with ginger-garlic paste, chilli powder, tomatoes and curry leaves until soft. In the meantime, juice the oranges – you should get about three-fourths of a cup of juice.

Boil the peel in hot water for a while and, using a spoon, scrape out the pith. Chop the peel and keep aside.

Mash the dhal into a fine paste once it is cooked. Add salt and orange juice, and place the cooker back on the stove but do not cover it. Add the chopped orange peel, and cook the dhal on a slow flame for a while. Then, add slit green chillies and coriander leaves and take off the stove.

FOR THE BAGHAR

Heat oil in a small pan until it is smoking hot. Toss in the red chillies, garlic and cumin seeds. Lastly, add the curry leaves. When the chillies are charred, take the pan off the flame and pour the baghar into the dhal. Cover the cooker immediately, to keep the aroma from escaping. Once the baghar has stopped spluttering, mix the ghee into the dhal and serve.

$\mathcal{M}$eat
and Poultry

'PETER ALWAYS LOVED TO HOST PEOPLE'

As I was researching the book, I spoke to Karki Hassan, who is Peter's cousin's wife and I call her Karki Bhabhi. She and her late husband, Abid Bhai, literally brought Peter up as one of their own when he was a young man, staying with them in Vizag at his first job. Before Peter and I were engaged, he wanted me to meet them and get their blessings without which, he said, we could not get married. I learnt later that he was joking but Karki Bhabhi still talks about how she remembers me as a 'terrified young lady with two plaits, who was afraid she would not be approved of'. Of all the meals I have made for her, she says her favourite is Shepherd's Pie. This is a note she shared with me for the book, about her memories of Peter and myself –

'People always say that behind every successful man is a woman but in the case of Peter and Doreen, I would say that they have both been very supportive of one another. Peter was a very devoted son and brother, and has remained devoted in all his roles. The Hassans are a very large Hyderabadi family with a very modern outlook and this has been so over the generations. Ours is a very multi-cultural, secular family and this has been true for generations. We like maintaining family ties and are very conventional only in this respect. And Doreen, with her Goan roots, fit right into the family from the start.

Peter has always loved hosting people. It is a part of his personality. I remember that at the start of his career when he had very little money, he would organize a tea party every couple of months and offer his guests cakes, something savoury and tea. He genuinely has always loved bringing people together. And Doreen has been a perfect partner for him. What has been very surprising for me is Doreen's ability to cook traditional meals. The Hassans are a foodie family – as we eat one meal, we're planning the next one – but Doreen was not a foodie when she married Peter. She doesn't even eat meat! So, it's only because of her wonderful personality that she has collected these precious recipes from aunts, cousins and other family members. She did it with so much grace, requesting them for their signature recipes, learning from them patiently and winning their generosity.

Doreen and Peter are now considered among the finest hosts in Delhi and are known for serving authentic, delicious Hyderabadi food. More than that, I think what they are loved for is their ability to bring people together over meals, and they do for the joy of it. Anyone can organize a meal and call people home but what makes their home special is the family's hospitality. Everyone makes you feel welcome. The little grandchildren are running around. The food is the best and the hosts are personally making sure that their guests are feeling at home. In a city like Delhi, which is a powerhouse, they have created a world for themselves.'

With Rt. Hon. Sir Anand Satyanand and Lady Susan

With Habib Rehman

With Pt Ravi Shankar Ji, Smt. Sukanya Shankar and Anoushka Shankar

COMING FULL CIRCLE

When I was thirteen, my father sent me off to the family's farm. He wanted me to learn how to cook and spend some time with our relatives. I was the youngest person there, and missed my parents and brothers. I remember calling my mother to tell her – 'You teach me how to cook, please! I just want to come home.' And I did go home very soon after but before I left, my aunt, Suraiya Hassan Bose, taught me how to make Kofte ka Saalan, which is one of her signature dishes. 'Beta, you must never use more than quarter kg of meat to make this dish,' she said to me as we cooked together. I promised never to, though I don't know why she said that and still have no idea.

Back in Delhi, my father wanted to know what I had learnt to make from Suraiya Apa and immediately asked me to cook it for a dinner party for fifteen people that he was hosting at home that evening. Of course, I had to use more than a quarter kg of meat, breaking my promise to Suraiya Apa almost immediately after making it. But this is life with my father – a full house and a full table, always. No one leaves our home without eating a meal. In fact, I don't think there was ever a time that it was just the five of us at the table. One evening, it was just the family sitting down to dinner and my father remarked – 'Who died? Why is there no one else joining us?' And just then, the doorbell rang and extra places had to be set for two friends who had decided to drop by.

I've been married for a little over two decades now and my own home in Goa is an extension of my parents'. There's always a meal for anyone who comes by and I love having people over. It's also the same spirit of hospitality that inspires Saligao Stories, a restaurant that I opened in 2016 in my great-grandmother's home in Saligao, Goa and where we serve both Goan and Hyderabadi cuisines. To me, it feels like coming full circle – from being that young girl who learnt to cook from her great-aunt, to now rustling up saalans, biryanis and curries as a restauranteur. Food truly is the greatest bridge and I believe I have been given a rare and blessed opportunity to be able to share our family's stories, through our favourite dishes.

Anisha Hassan Mendes

With President S.R. Nathan

Peter receiving the 'Order de Mayo – Officer of the Order' from Ambassador of Argentina, H.E. Ernesto Alvarez in 2012

TAS KABAB

INGREDIENTS

1 kg mutton (pasinda meat)
1 kg onions, finely sliced
1 cup oil
150 gm coriander leaves, chopped
8 green chillies, slit
4 limes, juiced
For the dough to seal the pan
As much wheat flour and water as you need

For the whole garam masala
10 cloves
6 cardamoms
4 1" cinnamon sticks
2 teaspoons peppercorns

METHOD

Mix the meat with salt and lime juice; keep aside for 30-60 minutes.

Heat oil in a pan and sauté half the onions until they turn translucent. Remove onto a plate lined with absorbent paper, and set aside.

Fry the other half to a crisp, golden brown in the same oil. Remove onto a separate plate lined with absorbent paper, and set aside.

Pour half a cup of oil into a large lagan or flat pan. Carefully arrange the meat pieces to cover the entire base of the vessel.

Cover the meat with both the browned, and slightly fried onions. As you sprinkle the slices, make sure you coat every inch of the meat.

Top the onion mixture with coriander leaves, green chillies, and whole garam masala. This has to be done in layers so please divide the ingredients accordingly. Do not use everything up in one layer

Repeat this process until you have used up all the ingredients.

Pour the lime juice and salt mixture, which the meat was marinated in and the remaining half cup of oil over the meat and its garnishes. Cover with water.

Seal the lagan with the dough; place on the fire with coals placed above and below it. You can also cook this dish in an oven, at 190° Celsius. Either way, it takes 30-45 minutes for the meat to brown.

Check the meat is cooked, allow the top to brown slightly.

Serve garnished with more chopped coriander leaves.

$\mathcal{S}$ANCHA GOSHT

INGREDIENTS

5 kg mutton, cut into strips

For the marinade

15 tablespoons ginger-garlic paste

3 tablespoons papaya paste

Salt to taste

To cook the meat

200 gm Bengal gram, ground and strained

100 gm yogurt

3 eggs

4 tablespoons oil

7 teaspoons chilli powder

6 teaspoons garam masala powder

2 teaspoons cumin powder

2 teaspoons coriander powder

1 teaspoon lemon yellow food colour

Handful of cashew nuts, ground into a paste

METHOD

Mix the marinade ingredients with the meat and keep aside for one hour. Drain off and discard any liquid that might be released at the end of the hour. Mix the rest of the ingredients together in a deep dish or bowl with a lid, and place the marinated strips of meat in this mixture.

Keep the bowl, covered, in the refrigerator overnight. When you are ready to cook the meal, heat coals on a sancha. Grill the meat strips until brown on both sides. Squeeze lemon over the grilled meat and serve hot.

$\mathcal{P}$ATTHAR KA GOSHT

INGREDIENTS

2 kg mutton (steak or pasinda cut)

2 tablespoons papaya paste

2 tablespoons garam masala powder

4 teaspoons black pepper powder

2 teaspoons black cumin seeds

2 teaspoons ginger-garlic paste

½ teaspoon all-spice powder

Salt to taste

METHOD

Wipe the mutton pieces with a wet cloth and then dry. Rub the papaya paste on the pieces and keep aside for two hours. Discard any liquid that might have collected. Mix in all the masalas with the meat; keep covered, overnight, in the fridge.

Heat a thick granite stone about 5" thick and keep the stone about 4" above coals to cook the gosht. Brush the stone with ghee and allow it to get very hot. At that point, place the meat on the stone and let it cook well on both sides. Brush more ghee on the stone as needed and repeat till all the meat is cooked. Serve garnished with onion rings and lemon squeezed over.

$\mathscr{S}$HIKAMPURI KABAB

This is a never-fail party favourite. You can make a big batch of the mince ahead of time to store in the freezer. The filling needs to be freshly-made, just before you fry the kababs. I make it for hungry children – and adults! – and it's also a great meal on the go.

INGREDIENTS

½ kg minced mutton

16 green chillies

16 pods of garlic

2 onions, peeled and left whole

2 onions, sliced and deep-fried

1 bunch coriander leaves

½ bunch mint leaves

12 cashew nuts

4 cardamoms

4 cloves

2 1" cinnamon sticks

4 tablespoons gram dhal

2 tablespoons poppy seeds

½ teaspoon black cumin seeds

For filling

100 gm yogurt or juice of two limes

½ bunch coriander leaves, finely chopped

1 onion, finely chopped

2 green chillies, finely chopped

METHOD

Roast the poppy seeds lightly; grind into a fine powder and keep aside. Take out a tablespoon of raw mince and keep aside.

Place the rest of the mince in a deep pan or vessel and add two whole onions, the green chillies, the pods of garlic, half a bunch of mint leaves, cashew nuts and four tablespoons of gram dhal.

Cover with enough water to boil in and add two tablespoons of oil. Bring to a boil, lower the heat and cook until the meat is done and all of the water dries up. In a separate pan, heat a tablespoon of oil and sauté the cooked, seasoned mince until all of the moisture evaporates.

Grind the mince along with the poppy seeds, a handful of fried onions, and all of the cardamoms, cloves, cinnamon sticks and black cumin seeds. At this stage, the mince can either be refrigerated to be used in a few hours, or frozen. You can make also oval shapes of the mince, skip the filling and fry them to make shami kababs.

TO ASSEMBLE THE KABABS

Thaw the mince completely, if it was frozen. Prepare the filling by mixing all the raw ingredients together. Shape a portion of mince into a ball. Create a hollow in the centre, place a little filling in it and wrap the mince around it. Flatten to form a round patty. Shallow fry the kababs in batches to ensure each one is well-browned on both sides.

Serve garnished with onion rings and, if you like, squeeze a little lime juice over the kababs.

NARGISI KABAB

INGREDIENTS

1 kg minced meat

¼ kg yogurt

¼ kg ghee

¼ kg onions

8 green chillies, finely chopped

6 eggs, hard boiled and shelled

2 bunches coriander leaves, finely chopped

1 bunch mint leaves, finely chopped

5 tablespoons chana dhal

4 teaspoons ginger-garlic paste

1 teaspoon chilli powder

1 teaspoon saffron strands, melted in a little water

Salt to taste

Roast lightly and grind together

6 teaspoons chironjee

5 teaspoons poppy seeds, soaked

1 teaspoon all-spice

Grind together

8 cloves

8 cardamoms

4 1" cinnamon sticks

1 teaspoon black cumin seeds

METHOD

Wash minced meat and grind well.

Roast and grind the chironjee, poppy seeds and all-spice to a fine paste. Add chana dhal and grind again to amalgamate.

Fry onions until brown and grind to a paste, using water.

Mix all the masalas and the yogurt with the ground minced meat. Coat the eggs with this mixture.

Grease a dish with ghee and place all the coated eggs in it. Pour the remaining ghee, chopped coriander and mint leaves, green chillies and saffron over the eggs.

Heat oil in a deep tawa or pan. Fry each egg until well-browned, and remove onto a plate lined with absorbent paper.

Cut each kabab into half, carefully, and plate on a bed of salad leaves.

$\mathcal{T}$ALA HUA GOSHT

INGREDIENTS

1 kg boneless mutton, cut into small pieces

2 bunches mint leaves, chopped

4 small bunches coriander leaves, chopped

6 sprigs curry leaves, chopped

2 cups water

½ cup ghee

4 tablespoons ginger-garlic paste

5 teaspoons red chilli powder

1 teaspoon turmeric powder

Salt to taste

METHOD

Mix the meat with ginger-garlic paste, turmeric powder and salt in a deep dish, and keep aside for at least 30 minutes. If you have the time, you can leave it to marinate for two hours, but not more than that. Mix half the chopped coriander, mint and curry leaves with the marinated meat. Cook the meat in a pressure cooker until the meat is tender and the juices dry up. This should take around 30 minutes.

Open the cooker once it is cool enough, heat ghee in a pan. Decant the cooked meat into the pan. Add in the chopped leaves that you had set aside earlier, along with green chillies, and red chilli powder. Let it cook on a medium flame until the gravy thickens. This should take about 15-20 minutes. Serve hot with rice or rotis of your choice.

$\mathcal{A}$DRAK LASSAN GOSHT

INGREDIENTS

1 ½ kg yogurt

1 kg boneless mutton

¼ kg ginger-garlic paste

2 cups oil

Salt to taste

METHOD

Clean and cut the meat into small cubes. Place the meat cubes in a strainer and wash thoroughly. Let all the water drain off.

Heat oil in a pan and sauté the ginger-garlic paste until it browns. Then add the meat, yogurt and salt. Cover and cook on a low flame until the meat softens and all the liquid dries up. You will need to stir the dish often to prevent the yogurt from sticking to the pan. The oil will rise to the surface towards the end of cooking and, if you like, you can drain it off. This dish does not have much of a gravy and you can either serve it with rice and dhal, or roll the meat into a paratha with some chopped onions and mint chutney.

Adrak Lassan Gosht

PALAK GOSHT

This is our family's version of a very classic dish. As with the Shahi Raan, it is best made for parties or other celebrations; serve with simple accompaniments to let the richness of the Gosht come through.

INGREDIENTS

1 kg mutton nalli and botis

¾ kg spinach

3 onions, finely sliced

5 cardamoms

4 cloves

1" cinnamon stick

2 heaped teaspoons chilli powder

2 teaspoons ginger-garlic paste

3 teaspoons oil

1 teaspoon coriander powder

½ teaspoon turmeric powder

Salt to taste

METHOD

De-stem the spinach leaves and roughly chop them.

Heat the oil in a pan and add the onions. When these start to turn brown, add in the whole spices, ginger-garlic paste and a few drops for water.

Sauté for a few minutes. Then add the powdered masalas, a little more water and add the meat.

Cook until there is no moisture in the pan.

Add salt, two cups of water and cover the dish. Turn the flame down and let it cook until the meat is nearly done. (If you prefer, you can do this in a pressure cooker.) When the meat is almost cooked, add the spinach leaves, cover the dish and let the greens wilt.

Serve hot with rotis.

HAHI RAAN

Impressive, delicious and decadent, this is an ideal dish for parties. I like serving it with accompaniments that will highlight and not compete with its richness – white rice or a simple pulao, Khatti Dhal and a kachumber.

INGREDIENTS

½ kg leg of mutton, washed and dried

½ kg tomato puree

2 cups sour cream

1 cup yogurt

1 cup oil

4 glasses water

20 almonds, blanched

4 teaspoons ginger paste

3-2 teaspoons chilli powder

2 teaspoons garlic paste

1 teaspoon garam masala powder

Salt to taste

METHOD

Prepare the marinade by mixing tomato puree, sour cream, yogurt, ginger and garlic pastes, garam masala and salt. Set aside.

Use a fork to prick the mutton leg all over. Place in a deep dish and coat it with the marinade. Cover and keep aside for four hours. The meat can be marinated overnight and it will actually cook better so if you can do this ahead of time, please do.

TO COOK

Heat oil in a thick-bottomed pan. Place the mutton leg in the hot oil and cook until it is light-brown in colour, turning it on all sides to ensure it is evenly cooked through.

Addf the marinade and water to the pan, lower the flame and cook the meat until it is tender. You might need to turn it over a few times to make sure it does not stick to the pan, or burn. When the gravy thickens and coats the meat completely, the dish is ready.

Garnish with blanched almonds and serve.

UTTON CHAAP

INGREDIENTS

1 kg pasinda meat
1 cup water
½ cup oil
2 tablespoons ginger-garlic paste
1 tablespoon coriander powder
1 tablespoon red chilli powder
1 teaspoon cumin powder

1 teaspoon black pepper powder
1 teaspoon garam masala powder
Salt to taste
For garnishing
½ kg onions, finely sliced
½ kg potatoes, finely sliced
3 tomatoes, finely sliced

METHOD

Wash meat well. Place it in a pressure cooker and add ginger-garlic paste, coriander powder, cumin powder, garam masala powder, water and salt. Pressure cook for three whistles and take the cooker off the flame. Once the pressure reduces, open the cooker and place it back on the stove, with the lid off. Cook on a low flame until much of the liquid evaporates, and there's about a tablespoon of gravy coating the meat.

Heat oil in a kadhai as the meat cooks on a low flame. Sauté the onion slices until they turn transparent. Remove onto a plate lined with absorbent paper, and set aside. In the same oil, shallow fry the potatoes until they turn crisp and light brown in colour. Remove onto a separate plate lined with absorbent paper. Finally, fry the tomatoes for a quick minute, just to soften the slices and decant onto a third, lined plate.

Take the meat out of the cooker and sauté it in the same oil until all the moisture dries up. Sprinkle with chilli powder as you sauté it.

Place the meat in a flat, wide dish. Cover it with the potatoes, then the onions and finally the tomatoes. This is traditionally served with rice and Khatti Dhal (page 50).

Tip: The leftovers from this dish can be made into a delicious meal. Cut the meat into small pieces and sauté in a pan with two tablespoons of oil. Break two eggs into the pan and scramble well with the sautéed meat. This can either be used as the filling for rolls, or served with parathas on the side.

GOSHT KI KADHI

INGREDIENTS

½ kg seene ka gosht, or mutton ribs

½ kg tomatoes, finely chopped

1 bunch curry leaves

1 bunch coriander leaves

10 green chillies

2 medium-sized onions, finely sliced

5 cups water

2 cups tamarind juice

¾ cup rice

½ cup oil

3 tablespoons coriander powder

3 tablespoons cumin powder

2 tablespoons chilli powder

2 teaspoons turmeric powder

METHOD

Wash the meat with the sliced onions and then drain. Add chilli powder, turmeric powder, salt and tomatoes. Pressure cook the meat till it is soft. Soak the rice in two cups of water for about an hour. Grind to a fine paste and add two cups of water.

Heat oil in a pan and add the meat. Sauté until the oil rises up to the surface and then add coriander and cumin powders, curry leaves and green chillies. Finally, add the tamarind juice and a cup of water. When it comes to a boil, pour in the rice paste in a slow stream. Mix well and simmer for 15 minutes. This dish is best served with plain white rice.

DHANIYA KHORMA

INGREDIENTS

1 kg mutton bone marrow and gizzards

2 large onions, ground

2 large onions, sliced

2 cups yogurt

4 tablespoons coriander powder, not roasted

4 teaspoons ginger-garlic paste

2 teaspoons chilli powder

For the garam masala

4 peppercorns

4 cardamoms

2 cloves

½ teaspoon black cumin seeds

METHOD

Heat oil in a pan and fry the onions until golden brown. Remove onto a plate lined with absorbent paper. To the same pan, add the meat and ginger-garlic paste; cover and cook for 20 minutes. Then, add the ground onion, mix well and cover again. Cook further for 20 minutes.

Sprinkle in the coriander and chilli powders. Add yogurt and a little water. Cook until the meat is soft and a rich gravy forms – this takes about 20 minutes. Add the fried onions and garam masala. Keep the dish on dhum for 5 minutes, and it's ready to serve.

Gosht Ki Kadhi

NALLI GOSHT

INGREDIENTS

2 kgs lamb shanks (about 15 pieces)

2 litres mutton stock

½ kg yogurt

150 gm onions, chopped

100 gm onions, finely sliced

100 gm Kashmiri chilli paste

75 gm garlic cloves

1 gm saffron strands

100 ml oil

1 bunch coriander leaves, finely chopped

1 2" piece ginger, cut into strips

8 green cardamoms

5 1" cinnamon sticks

5 cloves

5 bay leaves

5 drops vetiver

8 tablespoons ginger-garlic paste

4 teaspoons kewda water

4 teaspoons rose water

1 teaspoon garam masala powder

1 teaspoon black pepper powder

1 teaspoon green cardamom powder

METHOD

Fry the chopped onions until very crisp. Remove onto a plate lined with absorbent paper.

Fry the garlic cloves until they turn a deep brown. Grind these along with the fried onions with a little water to form a paste.

Heat oil in a pan and add the whole spices. When it splutters, add in the finely sliced onions and fry them to a golden brown. Then, add the ginger-garlic paste and the lamb shanks first. Mix well and add salt and chilli paste. Let the meat cook until the spices coat it – this should take about 15 minutes.

Mix in the browned garlic and onion paste and yogurt. Leave it on a low heat for 15-20 minutes. Pour in the stock and seal the pan with dough. Lower the flame completely and let cook until the mutton is tender. This should take 20-30 minutes. Check if the meat is soft, and if it is not, please return the pan to the stove for another 15-20 minutes.

Strain the stock, remove the lamb shanks and set them aside. Pour the stock into a thick-bottomed pan and return to the stove; let it reduce to the thickness you would prefer for the gravy. Check the seasoning and add the lamb shanks back in.

Sprinkle with the cardamom powder, garam masala powder, kewda water, rose water, vetiver and saffron. Mix well to combine and take the pan off the flame. Serve garnished with chopped coriander leaves and ginger strips.

KALI MIRCH RAAN

INGREDIENTS

2 raans, weighing about 2 ½ kg each

1 kg new potatoes

2 litres water

1 cup oil

5 level tablespoons ginger-garlic paste

2 tablespoons freshly ground pepper

Salt to taste

METHOD

Clean and wash the raans well. Boil the potatoes and let them cool. Peel and set aside. Place the raans in a large pan and pour in the water. Add salt and ginger-garlic paste.

Cook the raans on a slow flame until the meat softens and the water reduces to nearly ¾ its original volume. At this point, pour in the oil and bring back to a boil. When the liquid starts to boil, add the potatoes and pepper. Reduce the heat again and cook for 15 more minutes, until the gravy is quite thick. Serve garnished with more pepper, if you would like some more spice.

MUTTON ISTEW

INGREDIENTS

1 kg marrow bones

100 gm French beans

100 gm carrots

1 potato, cubed

1 cup milk

2 1" cinnamon sticks

4 cardamoms

4 cloves

2 bay leaves

1 tablespoon ginger-garlic paste

1 teaspoon pepper powder

1 tablespoon butter

1 tablespoon maida

Salt to taste

METHOD

Heat the butter in a pan and toss in the whole spices first. When fragrant, add the ginger-garlic paste. Sauté for a few minutes and then add in the meat. Once the meat turns brown, pour in three cups of water and let it come to a boil. Now, lower the flame and let the meat cook.

Stir the maida into the cup of milk and make sure there are no lumps. When the meat is nearly done, add the vegetables and cook until soft. Pour in the milk and maida mixture and stir well to help it amalgamate. The gravy will thicken in a few minutes. Add the pepper before you take the pan off the flame. The Istew can be served in deep bowls, with bread on the side.

Kali Mirch Raan

KOFTE KA SAALAN

INGREDIENTS

1 kg minced meat

¼ kg yogurt

2 large onions, finely sliced

½ dried coconut, roasted and ground

¼ cup oil

6 tablespoons Bengal gram, roasted and ground with very little water

5 teaspoons poppy seeds, roasted and ground with very little water

5 teaspoons chironjee, roasted and ground

2 teaspoons ginger-garlic paste

2 teaspoons red chilli powder

Salt to taste

To make the garam masala

10 whole cardamoms

6 cloves

3 1" cinnamon sticks

1 teaspoon black peppercorns

½ teaspoon turmeric powder

To make the green masala

1 cup coriander and mint leaves

5 green chillies

To garnish

4 green chillies, slit

Chopped coriander and mint leaves

METHOD

Grind the minced meat to a fine consistency without using water. This is best achieved on a masala grinding stone. Keep the mince aside. Again, on the grinding stone, grind the ingredients for the green masala, along with peppercorns and all the ingredients for garam masala. Scoop up into a bowl. Now, measure out half the paste into a separate bowl and keep aside.

Mix the chironjee, poppy seeds and chana dhal that you had roasted and ground earlier. Now, measure out half the mixture and place it in a separate bowl. In a large bowl, place the mince, one half of the green masala and one half of the powdered masalas. Mix the mince and the masalas as though you are kneading flour. This gives the mince a soft consistency and allows the ingredients to mix well.

Make small koftas of the mince and keep aside. Heat oil in a pan and fry the sliced onions until they turn golden brown. Then add the ginger-garlic paste, red chilli powder and turmeric powder; sauté well until fragrant. Now add in the second bowl of green masala and the second bowl of powdered masala. Add in the coconut. Continue sautéing the masala to allow the flavours to blend well. Then, add yogurt and mix well again. Once the oil rises to the surface, add the koftas, one at a time – they must not break.

Pour in two glasses of water and cook on a slow flame. If you need to mix the koftas in, do not use a spoon. Just hold the pan on both sides and gently shake it. When the gravy is thick and the oil rises to the surface again, add the green chillies, coriander and mint.

Serve with hot white rice.

SALIM BAKRA

From the time I became a proficient enough cook to begin hosting people, my day has always been punctuated by a call from my husband, announcing that he was bringing guests home for dinner. The numbers can vary from four to forty, or even more.

So, one day in 1986, Peter called me and said he had invited Mehdi Hasan, the famous ghazal singer, for dinner. He was to sing at our home, and there would be 100 guests in attendance. We had to serve a special meal. I decided to make a Salim Bakra, which is an entire goat, stuffed with chicken and eggs, and cooked to perfection. It is a difficult dish to make but it's perfect for special occasions and, of course, people cannot get enough of it.

As I prepared the goat, it occurred to me that I had come a long way from the young vegetarian girl who couldn't cook at all to this woman who was bravely and efficiently preparing an extremely complicated dish without batting an eyelid. The truth is that when I started cooking meat, I could not even bring myself to touch it, so I would pay my neighbour's maid a little money to clean and cut the meat for me. Making a dish like Salim Bakra by myself, therefore, was a proof of my journey. With 100 guests expected in a few hours, I couldn't dwell on my achievements for long but I still remember how good I had felt making Salim Bakra that day.

It's now a speciality of ours and Peter requested me to make it once for the Saudi Arabian ambassador, who was going to bring a friend along for dinner. I cannot remember the year now, but I will never forget the reaction of the ambassador's friend. When he saw the Salim Bakra, he could not believe that I had made it. Through the whole evening, he kept repeating to Peter – 'Your wife is a good woman.' It's become a favourite phrase of Peter's and he is still fond of calling me a 'good woman'.

If you are inclined to try making Salim Bakra – and I highly recommend you do – please ask for help and try it once before you cook it for an occasion. I would not advise you to experiment with this recipe. Follow the steps carefully, and don't be daunted by it. If I could master it, so can you.

INGREDIENTS

1 goat, weighing about 6 kg

2 to 3 small chickens

1 dozen eggs

1 ½ kg onions

1 kg biryani rice

1 kg yogurt

¾ kg ghee

¼ kg ginger-garlic paste

5 to 6 limes

8 teaspoons red chilli powder

2 teaspoons turmeric powder

Salt to taste

Flour kneaded into dough

to seal the pot

Grind together and keep aside

5 tablespoons chironjee

5 tablespoons watermelon seeds

3 tablespoons almonds

1 teaspoon saffron strands, powdered

Grind together and keep aside

15 1" cinnamon sticks

6 dry apricots

5 tablespoons raisins

5 teaspoons cardamoms

5 teaspoons black cumin

5 teaspoons mace

Grind together and keep aside

100 gm coriander leaves

50 gm mint leaves

6 to 8 green chillies

METHOD

Clean the goat, including the insides of the stomach. Apply the ginger-garlic paste, garam masala powder and salt to the insides and on the body of the goat. Keep aside for 1-2 hours.

Parboil the biryani rice and keep aside.

Hard-boil the eggs. Combine them with the parboiled rice. Divide this mixture into two or three equal parts. Stuff each chicken with one part and stich it up once it is stuffed. Roast the chickens in ghee on a large pan until half-done.

Place the chickens inside the goat and stitch up the goat.

Pour ghee/oil in a large lagan and roast the goat until it is slightly brown.

Mix all the ground masalas with the yogurt and pour the mixture over the browned goat. Seal the lid of the lagan with dough and keep on slow coal fire with coals above and below and cook till the meat is tender.

Place the goat in the centre of a large, flat dish. Open the stitches up, take the chickens out to serve.

HALEEM

This is another quintessential Hyderabadi dish, which is traditionally eaten during Ramadan. This recipe is our family's version of it. I often make it for dinner in winter because we find it to be a comforting, warming porridge. There are two components to this dish – the fermented wheat and the deeply flavoured Khorma. Make sure you eat Haleem as soon as it is made; you cannot store it even in the fridge for more than a day because the wheat will begin fermenting.

INGREDIENTS

2 kg boneless meat

1 kg wheat

½ kg sour yogurt

200 gm ghee

4 cups water

¼ cup oil

6 large onions, sliced

4 tablespoons cashew nuts

4 teaspoons ginger-garlic paste

2 teaspoons red chilli powder

1 teaspoon turmeric powder

1 teaspoon garam masala powder

Salt to taste

Lightly roast and grind together

8 cardamoms

2 tablespoons poppy seeds

2 tablespoons chironjee

1 tablespoon black cumin seeds

½ tablespoon coriander powder

Suggested accompaniments

A bowl of the whites of spring onions

A bowl of mint leaves

A bowl of radishes, sliced into strips

A bowl of fried onions

As many lemons as you'd like, halved

METHOD

Fill a large pan to the brim with water and soak the wheat in it overnight. The next morning, de-husk the wheat and pressure cook it until soft. Let it cool and then grind to as fine a consistency as possible. Ideally, it should resemble a thick porridge.

Heat oil and fry the onions until golden brown. Then, add ginger-garlic paste and chilli and turmeric powders. Fry until aromatic. Now, add the meat and fry until the water dries up. Then, add the masalas that you roasted and ground and allow the mixture to brown.

Add the yogurt and as much water as required for the gravy. I usually use five glasses of water. When the meat is cooked, add the garam masala and keep on dhum for a few minutes. Remove the pieces of meat and grind to a fine paste.

Heat 200 grams of ghee in another pan. Add the black cumin seeds and cardamom. Lastly, add the ground meat and gravy and mix well. Leave on dhum for 15 minutes.

Garnish the Haleem with fried onions and lemon juice. Serve with the accompaniments of your choice.

EHARI

This is a very traditional recipe for a nourishing soup made with trotters and tongue. Nehari is a favourite of Peter's, and I make it during the winters – as it is meant to be – and serve it with kulchas or Sheermals for dinner, because it warms you up and is very soothing. It can also be eaten at breakfast. Traditionally, Nehari was cooked all night in a large pot, but to suit modern kitchens and lifestyles, I have adapted the recipe to be made using a pressure cooker.

INGREDIENTS

2 dozen paya, or trotters, cleaned

2 dozen potla zaban, or tongues, cleaned

½ kg thick yogurt

2 cups chana dhal, ground to a fine paste with water

1 cup ginger-garlic paste

1 cup coriander leaves

1 cup mint leaves

1 cup oil

3 green chillies

3 limes

10 cloves

8 cardamoms

6 cinnamon sticks

3 tablespoons coriander seeds

1½ tablespoons salt (or as required)

1 tablespoon chilli powder

1 teaspoon turmeric powder

1 teaspoon pepper

1 teaspoon black cumin seeds

For the potli masala

3 large onions, quartered

5 cloves

4 cardamoms

3 cinnamon sticks

1½ tablespoons coriander seeds

1 teaspoon black cumin seeds

1 teaspoon whole black peppercorns

To Make the Potli Masala

Spread a large square of clean white muslin cloth – ideally measuring 12"x12" – on your work surface. Place the masalas in the middle of it and bundle it up tight to form a potli. Tie it with a clean white string – make sure it is tightly wound so that the cloth does not loosen during cooking. Leave a long thread of string which you can use to fish the potli out of the pot when you are done with it. This is the Hyderabadi equivalent of a bouquet garni.

METHOD

Clean the trotters very well. (Refer to page 30 for my notes on this)

Roast the trotters well on an open flame, using a pair of tongs.

Place the trotters and the tongue in a large pressure cooker and add twelve glasses of water. Add the potli. Cook on a slow fire until the meat is tender. This should take about 30-45 minutes.

Open the cooker when the pressure reduces and remove the potli. Using a pair of tongs, squeeze it to remove any juices. You can then discard the potli.

Heat oil in a large, heavy-bottomed pan. Add cardamoms, cloves, cinnamon sticks and three small onions, sliced fine. Fry until golden brown, and then keep aside in a bowl to use later.

Add the ginger-garlic paste, turmeric and chilli powders to the same pan. Stir until aromatic. Now, add the yogurt and keep stirring until it turns red.

Add the cooked meat along with its juices. Season with salt and lime juice. Cook for 10 minutes on a low simmer, allowing it to come to a boil.

Put in the paste of Bengal gram that you prepared earlier when it starts boiling. Stir to bring all the masalas together and continue cooking on a low simmer.

Add the chopped coriander leaves, chopped mint leaves and three green chillies when the gravy starts thickening. You can choose to slit them if you like, but that makes the dish spicier. So, if you prefer, leave the chillies whole. Take the pan off the flame.

Nehari is best served in deep bowls, garnished with a swirl of fresh cream, if you want to be decadent. Those who wish to, can add more lime juice to taste.

DHUM KA KHEEMA

My husband's younger sister Chintara, whom we call Chintu, is an excellent cook. She used to help their father in the kitchen when she was young and when I got married, we became friends.

Chintu was working as a teacher at the time and was not married, so we all lived together. Whenever we had people over for dinner, she would cook the meal but go to bed early because she had to go to work the next day. I would serve the meals. When I started cooking in Delhi, I would ask Chintu for family recipes. She taught me what she knew and it helped that Peter used to buy her sarees sometimes, as a thank you. Chintu lives in Canada now and while writing this book, I found many old notebooks in which I had written her recipes. This is one of those and is one of her specialties.

Chintara makes the traditional version, which is cooked on coals and I, too, prefer cooking it that way. For convenience, I have added a version that can be baked, which is easier and quicker, but achieves the same silkiness and deep flavours.

THE BAKED VERSION

INGREDIENTS

1 kg minced meat

¼ kg onions, sliced fine

¼ kg thick yogurt

½ cup oil

8 cardamoms

8 cloves

2 1" cinnamon sticks

4 heaped tablespoons gram dhal

2 ½ tablespoons coconut powder

2 heaped tablespoons poppy seeds

1 heaped tablespoon chilli powder

1 teaspoon turmeric powder

1 teaspoon black cumin seeds

1 teaspoon all-spice

Salt to taste

For the marinade

2 heaped tablespoons papaya, ground into a paste with salt

2 heaped tablespoons ginger-garlic paste

METHOD

Prepare the marinade by mixing papaya and ginger-garlic pastes together. Place the meat in a deep bowl and apply the marinade; keep covered in the fridge for six hours. When you are an hour or 30 minutes away from the meat being ready, start prepping the spices and masalas.

Heat oil in a pan and fry the onions until they turn golden brown. Decant them onto absorbent paper. Let the oil cool and pour into a bowl. Keep it aside – you will need this oil later.

Roast the poppy seeds and coconut powder separately. Grind together into a fine paste, using as much water as you need. Just remember not to make the paste too thin. Grind cinnamon, cloves, turmeric, cardamom, black cumin seeds and chilli powder together and keep aside. Take the marinated kheema out of the fridge and transfer it into a dish that is oven-proof. Mix in the prepared masalas and pastes and then the yogurt. Pour over the oil that you fried the onions in. Check the seasoning – you may want to add more salt – and keep aside, covered, for 30 minutes.

Preheat the oven to 150° Celsius. Bake the kheema until the top is brown and the marinade has dried up. This usually takes 45 minutes to an hour. Check it at the 35 mark. You may need to baste the meat in a greased pan on the stove to allow the marinade to be completely absorbed, and give the dish a very dry consistency, which is ideal.

Serve garnished with white onion rings, slivers of lime and mint leaves.

THE TRADITIONAL VERSION, COOKED ON COALS

INGREDIENTS

1 kg minced meat, from the thigh of the lamb

¼ kg yogurt

3 big onions, grated and fried

2 bunches coriander leaves, finely chopped

6 cashew nuts, ground to a fine paste

2 tablespoons Bengal gram, ground to a fine paste

3 teaspoons jalebi food colouring

2 teaspoons ginger-garlic paste

2 teaspoons chilli powder

Roast separately and grind together

4 heaped teaspoons poppy seeds

4 heaped teaspoons chironjee

1½ teaspoon all-spice

Grind, using water, into a paste

2 bunches mint leaves

25 peppercorns

10 cardamoms

5 1" cinnamon sticks

1 teaspoon black cumin seeds

METHOD

Do not wash the meat. Just wipe it with a damp cloth and store in the fridge for at least 30 minutes before you start preparing the dish. When you are ready to begin cooking, take the mince out of the fridge.

Place it in a deep dish and mix in all the ingredients – yogurt, onions, chilli and turmeric powders, and the ground pastes and spices. Add salt to taste and mix the ingredients well, like you are kneading a dough.

Grease a lagan and place the mince in it. Flatten it out and put a few drops of jalebi colour on top.

Squeeze the juice of a lime on top and drizzle two teaspoons of oil along the sides.

Make a hole in the centre and place two tablespoons ghee in it.

Heat a piece or two of coal (you will already have coal which is being heated to cook on). When the coal glows, drop it into the ghee or butter that you have placed in the dish.

Cover the lagan with a lid immediately, and hold the lid down tight. We do this to allow the smoke to permeate the meat, which adds depths of flavour. When the smoke disappears, remove and discard the onion skin and coal.

Seal the lagan with flour and place coals above and below it; cook for 35 to 40 minutes.

Serve the Dhum ka Kheema garnished with rings of onions, quartered limes and generous amounts of mint leaves on the side.

KALEJI GURDA

INGREDIENTS

¼ kg liver, cubed

2 kidneys, cut into 4 pieces

1 large onion, sliced

1 tomato, ground

4 tablespoons oil

2 teaspoons pepper powder

1 teaspoon ginger-garlic paste

1 teaspoon chilli powder

1 teaspoon garam masala powder

½ teaspoon turmeric powder

METHOD

Heat oil in a pan and fry the onion slices until they turn golden brown. Then add the ginger-garlic paste and turmeric and chilli powders. Sprinkle a little water and let the masala cook until it is aromatic.

Add the liver and kidneys; cook until the liquid dries up. Then, mix in the ground tomatoes. Simmer on a low flame until the meat is soft and well-coated with the masala. Finally, add pepper and garam masala powders and salt to taste.

SHEPHERD'S PIE – The Hassan Way

INGREDIENTS

For the kheema

1 kg kheema

500 gm tomato puree

250 gm onion

1 tablespoon ginger-garlic paste

2 teaspoons chilli powder

Salt to taste

For the mash

500 gm potatoes

250 ml milk

5 tablespoons breadcrumbs

1 teaspoon pepper

METHOD

Heat oil in a pan and sauté the onions till they turn a light brown. Add in the ginger-garlic paste. Mix in the chilli powder and kheema; cook on a low flame until the moisture in the meat dries out. Now, add the salt and tomato puree; cook until the mince is done. As the mince cooks, boil, peel and mash the potatoes. Set aside.

Heat butter in a pan and add the mashed potatoes. Pour in milk and mix. Add the pepper and salt. Mix well to combine and take the pan off the flame. Pre-heat the oven to 190° Celsius. Grease a baking dish with butter and decant the cooked mince into this. Top with the mashed potatoes. Bake for 15 to 20 minutes, until the mash is a deep brown.

Kaleji Gurda

Murgh Kari Patha

INGREDIENTS

1 kg boneless chicken, cut into 1" cubes

¾ kg sour yogurt, beaten

20 dry red chillies, broken into medium-sized pieces

4 fistfuls fresh curry leaves

4 tablespoons oil

2 teaspoons ginger-garlic paste

Salt to taste

METHOD

Wash the chicken pieces well.

Mix the ginger-garlic paste with the yogurt, and marinate the chicken in it for 2-3 hours.

Heat oil in a pan. Toss in the broken red chillies and one fistful of curry leaves.

Add marinated chicken and sauté on a medium flame until the meat is half cooked.

Add the remaining curry leaves and cook the chicken until the juices dry up.

Kadhai Murgh

INGREDIENTS

1 boneless chicken, cut into small pieces

¼ cup oil

6 onions, finely sliced

6 medium-sized tomatoes, finely chopped

6 green chillies, finely chopped

3 pods garlic, finely chopped

1 bunch coriander leaves, finely chopped

1 small piece ginger, finely chopped

1 teaspoon red chilli powder

Salt to taste

METHOD

Heat oil in a pan. Add onions, ginger, garlic and tomatoes; fry until the tomatoes break down and are well amalgamated with the onions.

Add the chicken and red chilli powder; let the flavours begin to meld for a while. Cover and cook until the chicken is tender.

Add green chillies and coriander leaves. Allow the gravy to dry up, and the oil to rise to the surface.

Garnish with more coriander leaves.

Kadhai Murgh

IMLI MURGH

We ate this dish nearly every day in my home, when I was growing up. It has very Goan flavours and is light, delicious and easy to make. Because it needs very little oil, it's also a healthy option and you can make it healthier by not frying the chicken at all, as I have explained in the recipe.

INGREDIENTS

1 whole chicken, washed and drained

5 whole dried red chillies

2 tablespoons oil

1 teaspoon whole black peppercorns

A fistful of tamarind, soaked in water and pulped

Salt to taste

METHOD

Rub salt all over the chicken – inside and outside. Set aside. You should have about three cups of tamarind water; if you don't, use more tamarind and water to make more pulp.

Heat oil in a pan and throw in the whole red chillies and peppercorns. Then, add the chicken and let it turn a light brown. Or, you can let it fry for longer and get very brown.

Pour in the tamarind juice when the chicken is cooked to your preference.

Cover and cook until the chicken is tender and the sauce has thickened.

Debone the chicken, except for the legs, to serve.

Serve Imli Murgh on a bed of lettuce, with boiled peas and fried potatoes as accompaniments. Or, place it on a bed of mashed potatoes and scatter peas all around.

URGH PASINDA

Mutton pasinda is a great favourite in our home but it can be a very rich dish. So, to preserve the flavours but make it lighter, I came up with this recipe, using chicken.

INGREDIENTS

1 kg boneless chicken

½ kg yogurt

½ kg oil

3 onions, sliced

3 green chillies

1 bunch coriander leaves, chopped

1 bunch mint leaves, chopped

2 teaspoons ginger-garlic paste

2 teaspoons red chilli powder

1 teaspoon garam masala powder

½ teaspoon turmeric powder

A pinch of salt

Lightly roast, and grind to a paste

2 tablespoons coconut powder

2 tablespoons poppy seeds

1 tablespoon charoli

1 tablespoon cashew nuts

METHOD

Wash the chicken pieces. Using a spatula, flatten each and keep aside.

Heat oil in a deep-bottomed pan, or tawa. Fry the sliced onions to a golden brown. Remove onto a plate lined with absorbent paper and let the fried slices cool slightly. Then crumble the fried onions into a rough powder and keep aside.

Strain the oil into a deep bowl. To it, add the chicken pieces, the roasted paste you made earlier, all the powdered masalas, yogurt, fried onions and ginger-garlic paste. Mix well.

Heat a pan. Arrange the chicken pieces on it and cook until tender and a thick gravy coats each piece. Mix in the chillies, coriander and mint leaves before taking off the fire.

TAMATAR MURGH

INGREDIENTS

1 chicken, cut into pieces

4 large tomatoes, pureed

2 onions, finely sliced

¼ cup oil

1" cinnamon stick

2 teaspoons ginger-garlic paste

2 teaspoons chilli powder

2 teaspoons garam masala powder

1 teaspoon black pepper powder

Salt to taste

METHOD

Wash the chicken pieces well.

Heat oil in a pan and add in cinnamon and onions; fry until the onions are golden brown.

Add the ginger-garlic paste, salt and red chilli powder. Sauté for a while, sprinkling a little water, if needed. Now add the chicken.

Leave the pan on a medium flame until all the moisture dries up. Pour in the tomato puree and cook until the chicken is tender.

Add the pepper and garam masala powders. The dish is done when the chicken is well coated with the masala and the oil rises to the surface. You can choose to drain off this excess oil.

Serve garnished with finely chopped coriander leaves.

SHAHI MURGH

INGREDIENTS

1 chicken, cut into 12 pieces	4 cloves
100 gm butter	2 cinnamon sticks
1 cup fresh yogurt	2 cardamoms
1 cup milk	2 bay leaves
½ cup water	3 tablespoons cashew nuts
2 hard boiled eggs, shelled	3 tablespoons almonds, blanched
1 bunch coriander leaves, finely chopped	1 tablespoon ginger-garlic paste
1 small onion, grated	1 to 2 teaspoons plain flour
1 sprig curry leaves	½ teaspoon cumin powder
6 peppercorns	Salt to taste

METHOD

Grind the blanched almonds with the cashews. Keep aside.

Place the chicken pieces and add grated onion, ginger-garlic paste, cumin powder, salt and a little water in a pan. Cook on a low flame until the chicken is tender.

Heat the butter in a separate pan when the chicken is nearly done.

Toss in the cinnamon sticks, cloves, cardamom, peppercorns, curry leaves and bay leaves. Once they stop spluttering, add the cooked chicken and the paste of almonds and cashews. Simmer for a while on low flame.

Beat the yogurt well and add to the pan. Cook for about 10 minutes more. In the meantime, dissolve the flour in the cup of milk. Slowly stir this paste into the pan to help thicken the gravy.

Cook for a few minutes and take off the flame.

Slice the boiled, shelled eggs into four long slices; garnish the dish with these and the coriander leaves.

MALAI KI MURGH

INGREDIENTS

1 chicken, washed and cut into 12 pieces
¼ kg fresh cream
1 cup water
¼ cup oil
2 onions, finely sliced

2 teaspoons red chilli powder
Grind to a fine paste
100 gm almonds
100 gm cashew nuts
50 gm raisins

METHOD

Heat oil and fry the onions until they turn light brown. Then, add the ginger-garlic paste and chilli powder; sauté until aromatic. Add the chicken pieces into the pan and cook for a while. Then, pour in as much water as is required to cook the meat, without too much gravy. I use three glasses of water.

Ready the dish for serving. Mix the ground almonds, cashew nuts, raisins and fresh cream in with the chicken and leave on slow fire until well-blended.

PALAK SOYA MURGH

INGREDIENTS

1 chicken, washed and cut into 12 pieces
1 cup yogurt
½ cup oil
2 bunches spinach leaves
1 bunch soya leaves
2 onions, sliced

2 cardamoms
2 cloves
2 1" cinnamon sticks
1 tablespoon ginger-garlic paste
2 teaspoons chilli powder
Salt to taste

METHOD

Chop spinach and soya leaves separately. Wash well, drain and keep aside. Heat oil in a pan and toss in the cardamoms, cinnamon and cloves. Add the sliced onion and fry until golden brown. Add the ginger-garlic paste and chilli powder. Sauté, sprinkling a little water at intervals. Now, add yogurt and let cook until the oil rises to the surface.

Add the chicken pieces to the gravy and cook for 15-20 minutes. Then, add the spinach leaves. When the chicken is nearly done, add the soya leaves. Cook until they blend with the spinach and the chicken is tender. If there is any extra moisture in the pan, allow it to dry up. Serve with hot white rice.

Palak Soya Murgh

KALI MIRCH MURGH

INGREDIENTS

1 chicken, cut into 12 pieces

2 cups yogurt

2 onions, finely sliced

3 tablespoons oil

2 tablespoons coriander powder

4 teaspoons black pepper powder

2 teaspoons ginger-garlic paste

1 teaspoon turmeric powder

1 teaspoon red chilli powder

1 teaspoon garam masala powder

Salt to taste

METHOD

Heat oil in a pan and fry the onions until golden brown. Add the ginger-garlic paste and turmeric and chilli powders. Sprinkle in a little water. Add the coriander powder and sauté until it turns a light brown.

Pour in the yogurt and cook until a gravy forms. Now, add the chicken pieces into the gravy and let them cook through. Then, add the freshly-ground pepper and garam masala powder. Keep on dhum for 5 more minutes. Serve garnished with finely chopped coriander leaves and some lemon juice poured over.

SHAHJAHANI MURGH

INGREDIENTS

1 whole chicken, washed and cut into 8 pieces

¼ cup oil

2 large onions, finely sliced

1 large tomato, finely chopped

1 large capsicum, finely sliced

12 garlic cloves, finely chopped

10 green chillies, finely chopped

1 bunch coriander, finely chopped

1 medium-sized piece ginger, finely chopped

3 cardamoms

3 cloves

2 cinnamon sticks

2 teaspoons coriander powder

½ teaspoon red chilli powder

½ teaspoon turmeric powder

Salt to taste

METHOD

Heat oil in a pan. Toss in cardamoms, cloves, cinnamon sticks and garlic; sauté for a minute or two. Add the ginger, green chillies, onions and salt. Mix in the chopped tomato and cook until it breaks down. Add the chicken and three cups of water, cook for 15-20 minutes.

Add the dry masala powders and make sure the chicken is coated with the spices. Do not add any water. Once the chicken is cooked through, add the sliced capsicum and continue to keep the pan on a slow fire until the capsicum slices soften.

Kali Mirch Murgh

AWABI MURGH

INGREDIENTS

1 whole chicken

3 tomatoes, pureed

3 eggs, beaten

½ cup thick yogurt

2 tablespoons ginger-garlic paste

1 tablespoons garam masala powder

1 teaspoon chilli powder

Breadcrumbs, to coat

Oil for frying

Salt to taste

For the stuffing

½ kg chicken mince

1 bunch spring onions, chopped

1 bunch coriander leaves, chopped

2 green chillies

1 teaspoon ginger-garlic paste

½ teaspoon garam masala powder

Salt to taste

METHOD

TO PREPARE THE CHICKEN

Wash the chicken and prick it all over using a fork. Then tuck the neck in the breast and keep aside as you prepare the marinade.

Mix together the ginger-garlic paste, garam masala powder, tomato puree, yogurt, red chilli powder and salt. Rub this mixture on the chicken – inside and outside – and allow it to marinate for 30 minutes.

TO MAKE THE STUFFING

Mix the mince with ginger-garlic paste, ground garam masala and salt. Heat a pan, add the spiced mince, and cook on a low heat until the meat is dry. Take off the stove, add spring onions and coriander leaves. Keep aside.

TO ASSEMBLE THE DISH

Heat a heavy-bottomed pan. Place the marinated chicken on it, and let cook until the marinade has dried up. Take the chicken off the pan, and let cool.

Stuff the chicken with the prepared mince, once it is cool enough to handle, and bind it with a sturdy thread. Dip the chicken in the beaten eggs, then in the breadcrumbs and again in the eggs. Deep fry until golden brown.

Serve garnished with tomato slices, onion rings and capsicum rings.

DHUM KA MURGH

INGREDIENTS

1 chicken, weighing approximately 1kg

¼ kg yogurt

2 bunches coriander leaves, finely chopped

1 bunch mint leaves, finely chopped

1 large onion, finely sliced

4 green chillies, slit

Juice of 1 lime

½ cup milk

1 dessert spoon ginger-garlic paste

1 teaspoon garam masala powder

1 teaspoon saffron strands

A few drops of lemon-yellow food colouring

Salt to taste

Flour to seal

Lightly roast and grind

1 dessert spoon poppy seeds

1 dessert spoon chironjee seeds

1 teaspoon all-spice

METHOD

Fry the onion slices to a golden brown. Remove onto a plate lined with absorbent paper, and let cool. Mash the fried slices into a crumble and keep aside. Strain the oil into a bowl.

Place the chicken in a deep bowl. To this bowl, add ginger-garlic paste, garam masala, roasted and ground spices, fried onions and the oil. Let marinate for an hour.

Dissolve saffron strands in milk in the meantime.

After an hour, place the chicken pieces on a flat pan or lagan. Add the marinade and sprinkle with the saffron-infused milk. Then, squeeze the juice of a lime and add a few drops of lemon-yellow food colouring. Mix everything well.

Seal the lagan with flour and place coals above and below. Cook on a slow and low flame. If you do not have a lagan, you can place the chicken pieces, marinade, milk, lime juice and food colouring in a thick-bottomed pan or vessel.

Cover with a tightly-fitting lid. Place the pan on the stove, and leave the flame on high for 10 minutes. Then, reduce it to a low flame and let cook for 15-20 minutes.

Check the chicken pieces for doneness. Once they are cooked, add chopped coriander and mint leaves and slit green chillies. Leave the chicken on dhum for a while, until the oil rises to the surface.

Serve garnished with coriander and mint leaves and, if you wish, more lime juice. °

Seafood

LIFE AT FAUST MANSION

This section of the book is especially dear to me because I have included several of my grandmother's recipes. I have so many precious memories of the meals she made us, and our life at Faust Mansion. While writing this book, I spoke with my cousin, Marie Campos; we had a long conversation, along with her husband Eugene, and our daughters, Karen and Anisha. Reminiscing about my life at Faust Mansion took me back to my childhood.

Faust Mansion was my world, and my school, St Anne's, was right across the street from home, as was the church we attended. My life was very simple and very regimented; we followed the same routine every day, waking up at 5.30 a.m. for church at 6 a.m., and it was lights out at 9 p.m. every night. (When I married Peter and moved into their home, I had to get used to a completely different routine – they sometimes ate breakfast at noon, and lunch at 5 p.m.! He still teases me about how much my life has changed.) My father had nine siblings, and Faust Mansion was where the family gathered during the summers and at Christmas. We had a large garden, full of trees, including mango, chikoo and jamun trees, which my cousins and I used to climb, much to our parents' and grandparents' concern. It was an old-fashioned house, with the kitchen outside of the main building and all our food was cooked over a slow fire for

many years, before the kitchen was moved inside the house.

The matriarch, Mama, ruled over the kitchen and she followed a set menu for all meals, except on Christmas or other special occasions. Breakfast was always parathas with homemade jams; the parathas were served in a silver box, which we all still remember. For lunch, there would be rice, dhal and a seasonal vegetable or maybe a fish curry and for dinner, we ate cutlets and bread. You didn't eat parathas after breakfast and rice after lunch, and all day long, there would be a pot of soup simmering on the stove that you could serve yourself a helping of, if you were hungry. We called it Mama's soup and any guest who dropped by was always offered a bowl of it. When I came home from school every afternoon, there was always something to nibble on – a sweet called dose, which was made of gram flour, and another called letri, made with coconut, were my favourites.

In the summers, Mama would sit at the head of the table and cut mangoes after lunch, passing plates of it down the table for all of us to enjoy. (When they were younger, Anisha and Nihal spent summers at Faust Mansion too, and they remember this ritual of eating sweet benishaan mangoes on hot afternoons.)

Sunday lunches were special and there were different menus – kofta curry (also called ball curry) and coconut rice; or tomato rice; or a very special chicken curry Mama used to make, which had slivers of fresh coconut flesh in the gravy; or chicken roast; or a delicious prawn pulao. Peter loved her

kofta curry and maintains that my version is not as good as hers used to be – Marie and Eugene had a good laugh about this as we swapped stories.

For the occasional feast or party, Mama made sorpotel and we all believe that hers was the best we've ever eaten. Birthdays were especially exciting for us as children because Mama baked her famous rainbow cake and made sandwiches with chutney, butter and vegetables or meat. Making those sandwiches was a collective activity, which made for a lot of fun and added to the festivities. Occasionally, we all also helped churn ice-cream at home in an old-fashioned churner; a lot of work would go into it, and everyone got a very small scoop in the end!

Christmas, of course, was the biggest celebration and the entire family gathered at Eugene's house after midnight mass. The adults would sing old Goan folksongs, and the children were encouraged to sing too, or dance. At 4.00 a.m., we would eat a fabulous dinner. Lunch was at Faust Mansion and it was Mama's special feast of all her signature dishes, especially sorpotel, without which it would not be Christmas. She made the cake at home too and there would be a variety of traditional Goan sweets as well as a carrot cake. Our grandfather used to make mango wine, which was always served at Christmas.

As young girls, one of our great thrills was to rush across the street to Garden Restaurant and bring some treats back home. We never ate there because we were not allowed to but there were waiters outside the restaurant, whom we called baharwalas, who would take our orders and then bring the parcels out to us. Marie and I can still list all the snacks we loved – Japanese cakes, samosas, Bombay baked beans and fresh mango juice. While visiting Hyderabad for the book, I went back to Garden Restaurant in Secunderabad after many years and was saddened to see that there is no garden left – it is a small cafe tucked into the side of a busy street. Faust Mansion also no longer exists, as the family has scattered across the globe. That green, quiet neighbourhood now only exists in my mind, and in the memories that I share with my cousins.

Our family was conservative and the girls were never encouraged to attend parties or go to movies with friends. Marie and I still giggle about how scared we would be to even ask Mama for permission if ever we were invited to a party. She would tell us to go ask our grandfather who would promptly send us back to her and that only ever ended in us staying home. Still, it was a wonderful life with very little to complain about. We were a close-knit family and remain one. And even though I might not have learnt to cook from Mama, I believe I still carry on so many of her traditions in my own home and life, passing on her legacy from one generation to the next.

MACHLI KA KHATTA SAALAN

In Hyderabad, we would traditionally use Murral for this dish, but you can choose to go with your favourite fish. And if you prefer, use fish fillets, which will be boneless.

INGREDIENTS

1 kg fish

¼ kg onions, finely sliced

¼ kg oil

¼ kg tamarind

¼ kg tomatoes, pureed

5 gm green chillies, slit

5 gm coriander leaves

4 cardamoms

1 cinnamon stick

To be ground together into a coarse paste

1 coconut, grated and ground

2 tablespoons coriander powder

5 teaspoons ginger-garlic paste

1 teaspoon chilli powder

1 teaspoon turmeric powder

For the baghar

1 sprig curry leaves

1 tablespoon cumin seeds

1 teaspoon onion seeds

½ teaspoon fenugreek seeds

METHOD

Clean fish, drain it and cut into round pieces.

Soak the tamarind in warm water and extract its juice.

Heat oil in a pan, and add a heaped teaspoon of cumin seeds and curry leaves. When these splutter, add the ground masala. Fry well.

Add tamarind juice and tomato puree.

Cook until all the flavours break down and a gravy begins to forms. Now, add the pieces of fish to the gravy. Do not use a ladle or spatula to mix it in. Just bring the dish to the boil, and using pieces of cloth or the handle, shake the pan carefully once or twice.

Lower the flame, and let the fish cook through. When it does, add in the whole garam masala spices, chopped coriander leaves and green chillies.

Serve in a deep, round bowl and garnish with more coriander leaves, if desired.

JHINGA AUR TAMATAR

INGREDIENTS

1 kg prawns, shelled and deveined

1 kg tomatoes, boiled and pureed

¼ kg onions, finely sliced

¼ kg oil

25 gm coriander seeds

10 gm cumin seeds

2 gm fenugreek seeds

1 dried coconut, grated

2 bunches curry leaves, chopped

3 2" cinnamon sticks

4 teaspoons ginger-garlic paste

2 teaspoons red chilli powder

1 teaspoon garam masala powder

A pinch of turmeric powder

Salt to taste

METHOD

Wash the cleaned prawns with turmeric and salt. Lightly roast coconut, cumin seeds, coriander seeds and fenugreek seeds and grind into a paste with water.

Heat oil in a pan and fry sliced onions until golden brown. Toss in the cinnamon sticks and sauté until fragrant. Then, add ginger-garlic paste, turmeric and chilli powder. Sprinkle in a little water and cook for a while.

Add in the prawns and toss well. Then, add roasted masala paste. Sauté until fragrant and add the tomatoes. Let prawns cook and when they do, add chopped curry leaves and garam masala powder. Lower the flame and continue cooking for 15 minutes until a thick gravy forms.

HUM KI MACHLI

This is definitely a good dish for a special occasion – it is full of lovely flavours and quite extravagant.

INGREDIENTS

1 kg fish

¼ kg yogurt

1 cup oil

1 small bunch coriander leaves, finely chopped

1 small bunch mint leaves, finely chopped

2 green chillies, slit

4 teaspoons ginger-garlic paste

2 teaspoons pepper powder

1 teaspoon garam masala powder

½ teaspoon saffron strands

Juice of one lime

Salt to taste

Grind to a fine paste

6 teaspoons chironjee

6 teaspoons almonds

4 teaspoons poppy seeds

METHOD

Clean fish and cut into large pieces. Wash and drain, piece by piece. Marinate with lime juice and ginger-garlic paste for 30 minutes.

Mix all the ground paste, pepper, garam masala powder and green chillies with the yogurt and apply it well on the marinated fish pieces.

Grease a lagan, which is a thick-bottomed vessel. (You can use a shallow pan instead, but make sure it is thick-bottomed.) Place the pieces of fish in the lagan or pan and pour oil over. Bake on a very slow coal fire or in the oven for forty-five minutes at 150° Celsius or until the fish is cooked.

Serve in the same lagan, which can be covered with foil. You can also decant it onto a flat platter. Garnish with the coriander and mint leaves, which you should chop just before, to keep fresh. You can decorate the sides of the platter with tomatoes, onions, leeks cut into flowers and/or halves of hard-boiled eggs.

BAINGAN MEIN JHINGA

INGREDIENTS

2 cups prawns, shelled and deveined

¼ cup oil, plus another 2 tablespoons oil

6 to 8 round eggplants with stems on

4 medium-sized onions, chopped

2 potatoes, cubed

Pulp of a lemon-sized ball of tamarind

Juice of 1 lemon

Salt to taste

Grind together into a paste

½ dried coconut, grated

8 whole Kashmiri chillies

5 peppercorns

1" piece cinnamon

3 teaspoons coriander seeds

2 teaspoons peanuts

1 teaspoon fenugreek seeds

½ teaspoon cumin seeds

METHOD

Keeping the stem intact, slit each eggplant twice to create four quarters. Place these quarters in a bowl of salted water until ready to use. Don't do this too much ahead of time or the eggplant quarters will lose their texture.

Heat two tablespoons oil in a pan and sauté onions until they are transparent. Add prawns and cook for 10 minutes. Take the pan off the flame at this point and mix in the turmeric, the ground paste and tamarind pulp. Allow this mixture to cool and then stuff the eggplants with it.

Heat a quarter cup of oil in a large, flat-bottomed saucepan that has a lid. Carefully arrange the stuffed eggplants on the surface, and add cubed potatoes. If you have any of the prawn mixture left over, add it in too. Cover and pour some water on the lid. Cook on a low flame until the eggplants and potatoes are well-cooked. Sprinkle lime juice over before you serve.

MACHLI MEIN JHINGE

INGREDIENTS

2 kg fish

2 teaspoons ginger-garlic paste

1½ teaspoons chilli powder

½ teaspoon garam masala powder

2 drops red food colouring

Juice of 2 limes

Oil for frying

Salt to taste

Ingredients for filling

1 kg small prawns

2 cups spring onion, finely chopped

6 tablespoons oil

2 teaspoons ginger-garlic paste

1 teaspoon red chilli powder

Juice of 2 limes

Salt to taste

METHOD

Clean the fish well and make slits on either side of the bone. Let any liquid drain out completely.

Prepare the marinade by mixing ginger-garlic paste, garam masala powder, red chilli powder, lime juice, salt and food colouring. Rub this mixture all over the fish and let marinate for an hour.

TO PREPARE THE FILLING

Sauté the spring onions in a pan. Add ginger-garlic paste, chilli powder, prawns and salt. Cook well, until the prawns are done and there is no moisture in the pan.

TO ASSEMBLE

Stuff the prawn mixture generously into the sides of the marinated fish. Wrap a length of strong thread all around the fish, to make sure the stuffing does not fall out.

TO COOK

Place the stuffed fish on a flat pan or baking tray. Bake at 150° Celsius until the fish is cooked. This should take approximately 45-60 minutes.

Do not try turning the fish because it will break – it will cook through on both sides without being flipped over.

TO SERVE

Scatter lettuce leaves, tomato slices, lemon slices and boiled egg halves around the fish.

JHINGA AUR PYAZ

INGREDIENTS

1 kg prawns, shelled and deveined

¼ kg leeks, finely chopped

¼ kg onions, finely sliced

30 gm ginger-garlic paste

2 bunches coriander leaves, finely chopped

3 green chillies, finely chopped

4 tablespoons oil

½ teaspoon turmeric powder

Salt to taste

METHOD

Wash the prawns with turmeric and salt. In a pan, heat oil and fry onions until transparent. Then, add in ginger-garlic paste and turmeric powder and sauté for a few minutes. Add in the prawns, toss to coat and mix; sprinkle in some water and let cook. When the prawns are half done, add the leeks and cook until the prawns are done. Garnish with the chopped green chillies and coriander leaves. Serve on a flat platter.

LAL MASALE JHINGE

INGREDIENTS

¼ kg prawns, deveined

2 tomatoes, finely chopped

1 onion, finely chopped

6 green chillies, slit

5-6 heaped tablespoons tamarind pulp

4 tablespoons oil

Salt to taste

Grind into a paste

1 fresh coconut, grated

30 fat red chillies

12 garlic cloves

½" piece ginger

4 heaped tablespoons coriander seeds

1 teaspoon cumin seeds

½ teaspoon peppercorns

½ teaspoon turmeric

METHOD

Wash the deveined prawns with turmeric and salt. Place the ground paste in a piece of muslin cloth and squeeze it over a bowl. Keep the extracted juice aside. This is the base of your curry.

Soak tamarind in hot water and pulp well to extract the juice. Heat oil in a pan and fry the onion slices until they turn golden brown. Add the chopped tomatoes and cook until these soften.

Add the prawns and slit green chillies; fry well and then add the ground coconut masala. Let the gravy cook until it thickens and the prawns are cooked. Pour in tamarind juice and bring to a boil. Serve in a deep bowl to get all the gravy in.

Lal Masale Jhinge

MACHLI MAHI QALIYA

INGREDIENTS

1 kg fish

2 gm patthar ka phool

2 medium-sized onions, finely chopped

2 fistfuls coriander leaves, chopped

2 sprigs curry leaves

¼ cup oil

4 tablespoons tamarind juice

3 teaspoons ginger-garlic paste

1 ½ teaspoons mustard seeds

½ teaspoon onion seeds

½ teaspoon turmeric powder

Dry roast and grind into a fine paste

2 tablespoons cumin seeds

2 tablespoons coriander seeds

2 tablespoons poppy seeds

2 tablespoons sesame seeds

2 tablespoons charoli seeds

¼ dried coconut, chopped

METHOD

Heat oil in a pan. Toss in mustard seeds, onion seeds and curry leaves; when these splutter, add the chopped onion and let it brown. Mix in the ginger-garlic paste and sauté until fragrant. Lowering the heat, add the ground masalas as well as the patthar ka phool.

Pour in the tamarind juice and when it comes to the boil, add the pieces of fish. Simmer on a low flame for seven minutes for the fish to cook through. Ideally, the gravy should not be a little thin – you can add a little water if it starts thickening before the fish is done.

Garnish with coriander leaves and take the pan off the flame.

Biryanis and Pulaos

HOW A BIRYANI CHANGED A LIFE

When Anisha and Nihal were little and we were still finding our feet in Delhi, my days were always packed. Between looking after the children, hosting people and running the house, I needed all the help I could get. At the same time, I was a consultant for Lepakshi, the Andhra emporium in Delhi, and I designed Indian and western outfits for them. It was especially challenging to keep Nihal busy and I was always trying to find a solution.

As it happened, a young boy from Tamil Nadu was brought to our house and we were told that he needed both a job and a place to stay. His name was Velu and he quickly became a part of our home, and then our family. I initially gave him only one job – to play with Nihal, but he was eager to help in any way he could, so he began working with me in the kitchen. Velu was an eager student who was quick to learn the recipes we cooked. Little did any of us know how it would change his life.

I am going to let Velu, who now lives in Washington DC, tell his own story, as he has written it:

My parents passed away when I was very young and I moved from my village in Tamil Nadu to New Delhi, in search of a job. When I first arrived, every day was a struggle and I did not even know how to speak Hindi. A friend found me a job with a Punjabi family but we could not communicate, so I quit in two days. My second job was at a restaurant in Munirka called Madras Restaurant. It was a lot of work for very little money and I realized that they were treating me unfairly because they knew I was desperate for a job. I spoke broken Hindi by then and had to stay on in a bad job because I could not find another. That first winter, I did not even own a sweater and was miserable. I finally asked a close

friend, Shanmuganathan, if he could find another job for me. I would do any kind of work, I said, and he took me to the Hassans' home.

We waited outside to see Ayya [Peter] and when he came home from work, Shanmuganathan asked if he would give me a job. The first thing Ayya said to me was, 'Have you eaten anything? Eat first, then we will talk.' At that moment, I felt like I was in heaven. I ate dinner and then Ayya asked my friend to translate the three rules of his house: 'No lying. No stealing. No alcohol.' He said that if I followed these rules, I could work in his house and he would make me a successful man. I started work that same day.

I learnt Hindi from Anisha and Nihal, and slowly started to help Amma [Doreen] in the kitchen. She first taught me how to make Dum Biryani, Pasanda Kabab and Tomato Chutney, and slowly I learnt all the other dishes that she used to make for parties. After about two-and-a-half years, one evening when Amma was in Hyderabad, Ayya asked me if I could cook dinner for his guests on my own. There were many VIP guests expected, including K.R. Narayanan, who later became the president of India. I said yes. When the party ended, Ayya told me that everyone had liked the food very much and that Mr Narayanan wanted to talk to me. He asked me if I would go to the USA with him, because he was being posted as India's ambassador there. He offered to take me along as a cook. When I first heard him say that, I was very scared and said no. I did not want to leave my home and go to a foreign country.

Ayya said to me, 'This is the best chance for a better life. Don't miss it. I will tell him to leave you in America to find another job when he finishes his term. Don't be scared to go with the ambassador. He's a nice man and he will take care of you. If there are any problems, I will send you a plane ticket and you can come back to India.'

I took his advice and worked for Ambassador Narayanan for three years in Washington. When he returned to India, I stayed in the US and found a job at Taj Mahal Restaurant in DC. The owner sponsored me so I could get my green card. In the meantime, I married my wife Shantha, who was from New Jersey. She is a wonderful wife and life partner. Our daughter Gowry was born soon after and I needed more income to buy a house. After working at the Indian restaurant for eight years, I quit, learnt how to cook American food and became a sous chef at the Embassy Row Hilton Hotel in DC. By then, our son Sekar was also born. At this time, the Hassan family visited me, which made me really happy. I worked at the hotel for eight years as well, but I needed more flexible hours since Shantha didn't know how to drive and my children needed someone to take them to and from school activities. I decided to drive a taxi, which I still do.

I have been able to give my children a good education and am so proud of them. They both went to college at University of Maryland. Gowry studied Early Childhood Development at Swansea University in Wales, UK, and is now a graduate of medical school, with plans to start her Paediatric Residency. Sekar earned his undergraduate degree with honours and spent his summers interning at Johns Hopkins, Northrop Grummond, and MIT. He is going to graduate school at Carnegie Mellon University in Pittsburgh for a PhD in Computer Engineering.

My life has been very successful since I met Ayya and Amma, and everything good that has happened to me has been their gift to me. I still think of Anisha and Nihal as little children, and it makes me very happy to see them as parents now. My family and I will never forget the Hassans and I always tell my children how important they are to me. Without them, I don't know where I would have been.

We have visited Velu several times in Washington and met his family, and he remains very special to us. He and his family are all American citizens now, due to Velu's hard work and belief that he will succeed where others may have failed. His success is testament to his courage and enterprise – he took a chance and made the best of it.

AHARI

Tahari is cooked by several communities across the country. This is the Hyderabadi version, which is lightly spiced and a meal in itself.

INGREDIENTS

1 kg Basmati rice
½ kg potatoes
10 cups water
8 medium-sized onions, finely sliced
8 green chillies
8 cardamoms

5 cloves
1 2" cinnamon stick
4 tablespoons oil
2 teaspoons turmeric powder
Salt to taste

METHOD

Soak the rice for about 30 minutes in cold water. Drain and set aside. Boil the ten cups of water to cook the rice in – cover, and set aside too.

Cube potatoes and soak in a dish of salted water.

Heat oil in a pan large enough to cook the rice in. Fry the sliced onions until golden brown. Remove onto a plate lined with absorbent paper, and set aside.

Add ginger-garlic paste to the same oil and sauté until fragrant. To this, add cinnamon, cloves, cardamoms, turmeric powder and potatoes. Continue cooking for about 3-4 minutes.

Bring the pan of warm water back to a boil at this point.

Add drained rice to the aromatics and mix well; lower the flame and let everything in the pan amalgamate for 3-4 minutes. Pour in the boiling water and stir only once. Cover and cook on a low flame until the rice is done.

Serve on a flat platter, garnished with fried onions and finely chopped coriander leaves.

CHANE KI KHUBOOLI

The flavours of this vegetarian dish are very similar to the Kachchi Biryani.

INGREDIENTS

1 kg Basmati rice

¼ kg Bengal gram

¼ kg yogurt

¼ kg oil

10 cups water

1 glass milk

5 large onions

4 green chillies, finely chopped

2 limes

A small bunch of coriander leaves, finely chopped

A small bunch of mint leaves, finely chopped

5 cloves

5 cardamoms

1 2" stick cinnamon

2 tablespoons ghee

2 tablespoons ginger-garlic paste

2 teaspoons red chilli powder

1 teaspoon turmeric powder

½ teaspoon saffron strands

METHOD

Wash and cook the lentils until tender but firm.

Wash rice well and soak in cold water for 30 minutes. Drain and set aside.

Heat oil and fry onions until golden brown in a pan large enough to cook the lentils. Remove onto a plate lined with absorbent paper, and set aside.

Add ginger-garlic paste to the same oil that you fried onions in, and let cook until fragrant. Then, add chilli powder and turmeric powder and sauté for a while to let the flavours amalgamate. Add the yogurt and sauté well. Now, add in the cooked lentils, chopped coriander leaves, green chillies, mint leaves and lime juice. Cook until the yogurt blends with the lentils.

Put ten cups of water to the boil. When it comes to a rolling boil, add in the drained rice and cook until three-fourths done.

Grease a large heavy-bottomed pan with a tablespoon of ghee and spoon a layer of rice over the bottom. Spoon the lentil mixture over the rice. Then, sprinkle some fried onions, chopped coriander and mint leaves, two green chillies and cover with more rice.

Repeat until you have used all the rice and lentils, and finally pour two tablespoons of ghee over the top.

Melt saffron in half a glass of milk and sprinkle over the rice. Sprinkle the other half-glass of plain milk too.

Seal the pan and cook on a high flame for 15 minutes and then on a low flame for 20 minutes.

Serve garnished with fried onions and cut coriander and mint leaves.

$\mathcal{S}$AFED PULAO

This is a dish that looks lovely and is full of unusual flavours. It is the centrepiece of my White Menu (Page 208). Serve it on a silver platter, if you can, to showcase its delicate beauty.

INGREDIENTS

1 kg Basmati rice

1 kg mutton – adla cut, chops, marrow bones

½ kg yogurt

¼ kg onions

¼ kg oil

½ litre milk

100 gm fresh cream

10 cups water

1 small bunch coriander leaves

1 small bunch mint leaves

6 green chillies

6 cardamoms

3 bay leaves

2 1" cinnamon sticks

3 tablespoons ghee

4 teaspoons ginger-garlic paste

1 teaspoon black cumin seeds

Salt to taste

METHOD

Wash rice and soak for 30 minutes in cold water.

Wash meat and marinate for 30 minutes with ginger-garlic paste.

Grind the coriander and mint leaves into a paste.

Add this paste, yogurt, fresh cream and salt to taste to the meat. In a pan large enough to cook the pulao in, put water to the boil with cardamoms, cinnamon sticks, black cumin seeds and bay leaves.

When it comes to a rolling boil, add the rice and cook till it is three-fourths done.

Drain through a strainer and spread out on a large flat plate.

Heat oil in a pan, large enough to cook the meat in, and fry onions until golden brown. Add the marinated meat and green chillies. Pour in two to three cups of water to form a thick gravy and cook until the meat is tender. Take the pan off the stove when the meat is cooked.

Layer the partly-cooked rice over the meat. Sprinkle milk over the rice and dot with three tablespoons of ghee.

Seal the pan and cook over high flame for 10 minutes and on a low flame for about 20 minutes, until the rice is done.

Serve garnished with fried onions.

CHILLAV

INGREDIENTS

1 kg Basmati rice
1 kg minced meat
¼ kg yogurt
¼ kg coriander leaves
¼ kg onions, finely sliced
10 cups water

½ cup oil
6 green chillies
Juice of 2 limes
2 tablespoons ginger-garlic paste
2 teaspoons red chilli powder
1 teaspoon turmeric powder

METHOD

Soak the rice for about half an hour in cold water. Drain and set aside. Boil the water to cook the rice in – cover, and set aside too.

In a pan large enough to cook the rice in, heat oil and fry sliced onions until golden brown. Add ginger-garlic paste and chilli and turmeric powders; cook until fragrant.

Mix in the yogurt and stir to combine for a few minutes. Then, add the minced meat. Cook until the raw smell of the meat disappears. The mince must also blend well with the yogurt.

In the meantime, put the pan of water back to the boil.

Add to the pan of meat, rice and mix well. When the mixture begins to brown, pour in the boiling water and stir well. Cover and cook on a low flame.

Add chopped coriander leaves, green chillies and lime juice when there is very little liquid in the pan. Cook until there is no liquid in the pan.

Serve garnished with chopped coriander leaves.

NIMBU ZAFRANI PULAO

INGREDIENTS

1 kg Basmati rice

10 cups chicken stock, made with the bones of 1 chicken

1 cup coriander leaves, finely chopped

¾ cup lemon juice

4 medium-sized onions

1 sprig curry leaves

3 tablespoons oil

2 tablespoons ghee

2 tablespoons lemon rind, grated

3 teaspoons ginger-garlic paste

1 teaspoon saffron strands

Salt to taste

METHOD

Prepare chicken stock by pressure cooking the chicken bones in about eleven cups of water.

Melt the saffron and mix it with the stock. Set aside.

Heat oil and ghee in a pan, large enough to cook the rice in.

Add onions, ginger-garlic paste and curry leaves. Lower the flame and let the onions turn golden brown. Then add rice and lemon rind.

Mix well, and let cook for a few minutes before pouring in the chicken stock. Cover and cook until the liquid is nearly drying up. At that point, put in the lemon juice and coriander leaves.

Simmer for another 5-7 minutes until the rice is cooked and there is no liquid in the pan.

Serve garnished with finely chopped coriander leaves.

KACHCHI BIRYANI

After my children and I returned home to Delhi from that early trip to Hyderabad, and my cooking lesson from Phuppu Jani, Peter began calling people over for dinner often. One evening, I decided to make the mutton biryani that I had learnt. To make it less stressful for myself, I didn't tell Peter of my plan. I made it when he was at work. Because I had been watching the cooks – first the lady, and now the man Peter had found – at home in Delhi more closely, I knew my way around the kitchen by now. When Peter came home, I told him that I had ordered it in. He had many questions about where it was from but I managed to evade all of them. I served the biryani and our guests seemed to like it. At the end of the evening, I told Peter I had made it and he said – 'Don't tell me! I don't believe it. It was very good, very, very good.' Peter was always so encouraging, which motivated me to try my hand at more dishes and slowly, I discovered a real love for cooking, which holds true till this day.

INGREDIENTS

1 kg Basmati rice

1 kg adla mutton (meat from the shin bone)

½ kg oil

½ kg onions, finely sliced

¼ kg milk

¼ kg yogurt

3 bunches coriander leaves, finely chopped

2 bunches mint leaves, finely chopped

10 green chillies, slit

3 limes

5 cardamoms

3 1" cinnamon sticks

3 bay leaves

2 tablespoons ginger-garlic paste

3 teaspoons green papaya paste

2 teaspoons black cumin seeds

1 teaspoon saffron strands

Salt to taste

Grind to a fine powder

12 cardamoms

6 cloves

6 1" sticks cinnamon

METHOD

Fry the onions until golden brown. Remove onto a plate lined with absorbent paper, and let cool. Then, mash into a crumbly powder and keep aside.

Pour the oil out of the pan, sieve and set aside too.

Rub the meat with a halved onion as you wash it. Drain off any juices that are released. In the pan in which you are going to cook the meat, marinate it with the papaya paste for about 2 hours. Drain off any more juices that collect in the pan. Now, smear the ginger-garlic paste and two tablespoons of salt on the meat. Set aside for another hour. Add yogurt to the marinated meat and leave for another half hour.

Finally, mix in the masala you ground up along with the chopped coriander and mint leaves, fried onions and green chillies with the meat. Pour the oil you had set aside into the pan.

Heat water with cardamoms, cinnamon sticks, black cumin seeds and bay leaves in a separate large pan. When it comes to a rolling boil, add in the rice and cook until half done. Drain the rice but leave some water in there – do not let it dry out completely.

Layer the parboiled rice over the marinated meat.

Dissolve the saffron in the milk and sprinkle this mixture over the rice and meat. Dot with about four tablespoons of ghee or oil.

Seal the pan with dough and place it on a high flame for about fifteen minutes. Then lower the flame and cook for another 30 minutes.

Before you serve, use a very large spatula or a small plate to cut through the biryani from the top to the bottom but do not disturb the layering. It does not need to be mixed.

Garnish with fried onions, coriander and mint leaves.

UKKI BIRYANI

INGREDIENTS

1 kg Basmati rice

1 kg adla mutton (meat from the shin bone)

½ kg yogurt

¼ kg oil

1 glass milk

½ cup ginger-garlic paste

4 bunches coriander leaves

2 bunches mint leaves

8 green chillies

2 large onions, finely sliced

3 limes

10-12 cardamoms

4 cloves

1 2" cinnamon stick

2 teaspoons black cumin seeds

2 teaspoons chilli powder

1 teaspoon turmeric powder

1 teaspoon saffron strands

Salt to taste

METHOD

When you buy the meat, get it cut into medium-sized pieces. Wash the rice and soak for at least 30 minutes in cold water.

Mix meat with ginger-garlic paste, turmeric powder, two teaspoons of salt and yogurt. Set aside for at least an hour. You can leave it to marinate for 2-3 hours or overnight.

Heat oil in a large pan and fry onions until golden brown. Remove onto a plate lined with absorbent paper, and set aside. To the same oil, add six cardamoms and a teaspoon of black cumin seeds. When these splutter, add the meat and cook until a thick gravy forms. This takes about 30-45 minutes.

Add two teaspoons of chilli powder just as the meat is nearly done, and leave the pan on the stove until the oil rises to the surface. Put 10-12 cups water to the boil, with cloves, cinnamon sticks, six cardamoms and a teaspoon of black cumin seeds. Once it comes to a rolling boil, add the drained rice to it and cook until three-fourths done.

Pass the cooked rice through a strainer, making sure you retain the whole spices and about half a glass of water. Do not dry out the rice completely. Grease a pan and layer half the rice on the bottom. Then spread a layer of meat. Sprinkle half the fried onions, half of the chopped coriander and mint leaves, green chillies and the juice of three limes. Repeat all three layers.

Cover with the remaining rice and pour over the oil that you drained off the meat curry.

Mix saffron in milk and sprinkle over the rice. Seal the pan and cook on dhum for 15 minutes.

Before you serve, use a very large spatula or a small plate to cut through the biryani from the top to the bottom. This makes it easier for everyone to serve themselves. Garnish with the remaining fried onions and coriander and mint leaves.

HYDERABADI MUTTON PULAO

INGREDIENTS

1 kg adla meat (meat from the shin bone)

1 kg Basmati rice

¼ kg oil

10 cups water

1 cup milk

½ cup yogurt

1 bunch coriander leaves, finely chopped

1 bunch mint leaves, finely chopped

1 large onion, finely sliced

1 lime, juiced

6-8 green chillies, slit lengthwise

10 peppercorns

6 cloves

3 green cardamoms

3 1" cinnamon sticks

1 black cardamom

3 tablespoons fresh cream

1 heaped tablespoon coriander powder

2 teaspoons black cumin seeds

2 teaspoons ginger paste

1 teaspoon garlic paste

1 teaspoon saffron strands

Salt to taste

Roast lightly and grind

2 teaspoons poppy seeds

1 teaspoon chironjee

For the marinade

½ cup yogurt

1 heaped tablespoon dhaniya powder

2 teaspoons ginger paste

2 teaspoons poppy seeds

1 teaspoon garlic paste

1 teaspoon charoli

METHOD

TO PREPARE THE MUTTON

Mix the roasted and ground khus khus with the marinade ingredients and three cinnamon sticks, ten peppercorns and the black cardamom. Apply this marinade to the meat and leave for at least an hour. Place the mutton in a pan on a slow flame and cook until the meat softens. At that point, take the pan off the flame. If any oil has risen to the surface, drain it off and set it aside.

TO COOK THE RICE

Boil water with three cinnamon sticks, three cardamoms, six cloves, a heaped teaspoon black cumin seeds and salt to taste. When the water comes to a rolling boil, add rice and cook until three-fourths done.

In a large greased dish, layer half the rice. Top it with the cooked mutton. Sprinkle with the remaining black cumin seeds, lime juice, four green chillies and some of the coriander and mint leaves. Cover with the remaining rice. Mix salt in two cups of water and sprinkle over.

Mix the saffron in one cup of milk. Sprinkle this, and the oil you drained off the mutton, over the rice. Seal the pan and keep on a low flame for 15 minutes.

Serve garnished with fried onions, coriander leaves and whole mint leaves.

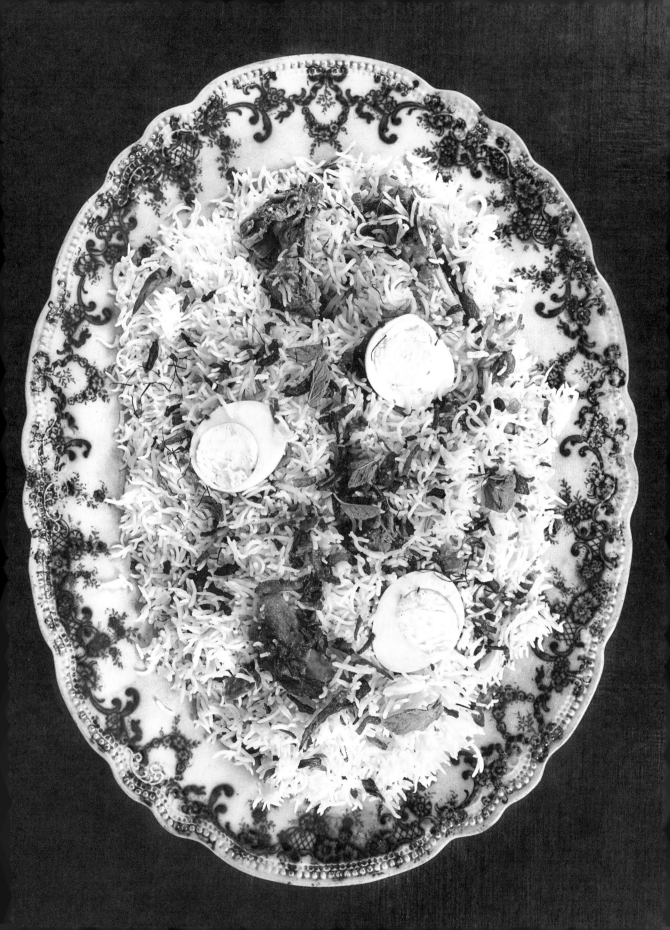

KAJU PULAO

INGREDIENTS

1 kg Basmati rice
250 gm onions, finely sliced
250 gm yogurt
200 gm cashew nuts
10 cups water
1 glass milk
1 bunch coriander leaves, finely chopped
1 bunch mint leaves, finely chopped
6 green chillies, slit
2 limes

4 cardamoms
2 1" cinnamon sticks
4 tablespoons ghee or oil
2 teaspoons chilli powder
2 teaspoons ginger-garlic paste
1 teaspoon turmeric powder
1 teaspoon saffron strands
½ teaspoon garam masala powder
½ teaspoon black cumin seeds
Salt to taste

METHOD

Heat oil in a frying pan and fry onions until light brown in colour. Remove onto a plate lined with absorbent paper, and set aside. In the same oil, lightly fry the cashew nuts; remove those onto a separate plate lined with absorbent paper.

Pour off the oil, sieve it and set it aside.

Mix the fried cashews with yogurt, half the fried onions, chilli powder, ginger-garlic paste, turmeric, salt and garam masala powder in a bowl.

Put water to boil in a pan large enough to cook the rice in. When it comes to a rolling boil, add rice, cardamom, cinnamon, black cumin seeds, half the coriander and mint leaves, three green chillies and salt.

Cook until the rice is three-fourths done. In the meantime, mix the saffron into the milk.

Take the pan off the heat and decant the rice to a plate or platter.

In the same pan, layer half the rice on the bottom. Then, pour over the yogurt-cashew mixture. Add the remaining coriander and mint leaves, three green chillies and some of the fried onions. Pour over the oil that you kept aside earlier.

Cover with the remaining rice and sprinkle the saffron-infused milk over the top. Dab with about four tablespoons of ghee or oil. Seal the pan and keep on dhum for about 20 minutes.

Serve garnished with fried onions and, if you like, chopped coriander and mint leaves.

 NAWABI PULAO

INGREDIENTS

1 kg adla mutton (from the shin bone)

750 gm Basmati rice

10 cups water

1 cup yogurt, beaten

½ cup milk

5-6 medium-sized onions

10 peppercorns

10 apricots

6 red chillies

6 cardamoms

2 1" cinnamon sticks

1 tablespoon ginger-garlic paste

2 teaspoons garam masala powder

1 teaspoon black cumin seeds

1 teaspoon saffron strands

1 teaspoon turmeric powder

A handful each of almonds, cashew nuts, chironjee and raisins

Ghee

Salt to taste

METHOD

Wash the rice and set aside to soak in cold water for 30 minutes. Wash the mutton and set aside.

Fry onions until golden brown. Remove onto a plate lined with absorbent paper and let cool. Grind the fried onions and red chillies to a fine paste. Mix this paste with the beaten yogurt, ginger-garlic paste, turmeric and salt to taste. Marinate the mutton in the mixture for 90 minutes.

Heat five tablespoons of ghee in a frying pan and roast almonds, cashew nuts, chironjee and raisins. At the end of 90 minutes, heat 2 ½ tablespoons of oil or ghee in a pressure cooker. Add in the marinated mutton and cook until it softens.

Drain the soaked rice through a strainer and set aside. Put water to the boil. Dissolve saffron in milk. In a separate, large pan, heat a little ghee or oil, and add peppercorns, cinnamon sticks, cardamoms and black cumin seeds. When these splutter, add the drained rice and sauté for a while.

Pour in the boiling water and salt to taste. Cook until the rice is done. Spread the cooked rice on a plate or platter; pick out the spices and discard.

Take another pan large enough to cook the rice and mutton in, and grease the bottom and sides with ghee. Pour in the prepared mutton and sprinkle garam masala powder over it. Cover with the rice and dot with two tablespoons of ghee.

Make four deep holes in the layers and sprinkle the saffron-infused milk through these. Sprinkle the fried nuts and fried onions over the rice.

Seal the pan and cook on a low flame for 20 minutes.

Serve on a platter, garnished with chopped coriander and mint leaves.

*R*otis

$\mathcal{B}$ESAN KI ROTI

This is a rather unusual roti, and is delicious, especially when served with vegetarian dishes and a range of pickles and chutneys. I also like serving this at parties, just for a change from the usual suspects.

INGREDIENTS

150 ml water

100 gm wholemeal flour

75 gm gram flour

2 green chillies

1 small onion, finely chopped

½ bunch coriander leaves, finely chopped

2 teaspoons ghee

½ teaspoon salt

METHOD

Sift the wholemeal flour and gram flour together into a mixing bowl. Add salt, onion, coriander leaves and green chillies. Using enough water, form a soft dough. Cover and set aside for 15-20 minutes.

Knead well, again, and divide into six equal portions. Roll each out into a roti on a surface that has been lightly dusted with flour.

Heat a flat tawa or pan. Working with one roti at a time, roast both sides, greasing each as it is done.

Serve hot.

ESHMI PARATHA

This is a very rich paratha – there are eggs and milk in the dough, and it is deep-fried. It pairs very well with Safed Mirchi ka Saalan and Tamatar ka Kut. In our home, every time there is a special request for a menu of treats, these three dishes are always included. I also serve these parathas at parties and guests love them.

INGREDIENTS

1 kg maida, or plain flour

1 litre oil

750 ml milk

2 eggs

1 tablespoon sugar

¾ teaspoon salt

METHOD

Sift the flour into a mixing bowl and add sugar and salt. Make a well in the centre, and gently fold in eggs and milk, mixing with your fingers as you do. Knead well to form a firm but soft dough.

Cover and allow to stand for about 30 minutes.

Divide the dough into equal portions and roll each into what looks like a long snake.

Roll this into a coil, dusting with flour as you do. Place this coil on a surface dusted with flour, and roll out into a round shape.

Heat a tawa or flat pan until it is very hot. Dry roast each roti well – do not add any oil or ghee right now.

When all the rotis are roasted, heat the oil in a kadhai or wok. Deep fry each roti, and remove onto a plate or platter lined with absorbent paper.

Cut into halves or fours and serve hot.

OGHINI ROTI

An old-fashioned roti, it is rich in flavour, making it a perfect choice to take along while travelling. A Roghini Roti fills you up, and all you need is a simple kheema or scrambled eggs to eat it with.

INGREDIENTS

300 ml milk

225 gm wholemeal flour

1 tablespoon ghee

½ teaspoon salt

METHOD

Place the flour and salt in a mixing bowl. Make a well in the centre and slowly fold in the ghee and the milk. Knead to a soft dough and let it stand for about 10-15 minutes.

Divide the dough into ten equal portions. Roll each out into a round shape, dusting flour on it. Using a fork, pierce the roti in whichever pattern you want. On a hot tawa or flat pan, roast the roti on both sides. Now, apply ghee on one side and cook it. Repeat on the other side.

ETHI ROTI

These rotis are especially delicious when served with meat dishes.

INGREDIENTS

2 cups wheat flour

2 bunches fenugreek leaves, finely chopped

1 bunch coriander leaves, finely chopped

4 green chillies, finely chopped

METHOD

Sift the flour into a bowl and mix in chopped fenugreek and coriander leaves, green chillies and salt. Add enough water and ghee or oil to make a soft dough.

Divide into twelve portions and roll out the rotis. Cook as you would regular rotis, and brush each with a little ghee before you serve.

ZAFFRANI SHEERMAL

This is a very special bread that is traditionally eaten with kababs. It is very tasty and because sheermal are not very large, you can end up eating more than you thought you would.

INGREDIENTS

1 kg maida, or plain flour
1 kg milk
½ kg ghee
1 teaspoon salt

1 teaspoon sugar
A drop of kewra essence
A drop of rosewater
A few strands of saffron

METHOD

Heat saffron on a dry tawa or flat pan. Add it to ¼ cup water and let it melt. Set aside.

Place the flour, salt and sugar in a mixing bowl and make a well in the centre. Slowly mix in the ghee, milk, kewra essence and rosewater. Knead well.

Cover and allow to stand for about 30 minutes.

Divide the dough into smaller equal portions. Roll these out into little round shapes, about 4" in diameter.

Lightly brush each with a little ghee or oil. You can cook these rotis in the tandoor or a preheated oven at 150°-200° Celsius.

When they are nearly done, sprinkle them with saffron water and cook until done.

Pickles

and Chutneys

IRCHI PASTE

INGREDIENTS

4 tablespoons onions, chopped and fried

4 tablespoons red chilli powder

3 tablespoons oil

1 tablespoon ginger-garlic paste

Juice of 2 limes

Salt to taste

METHOD

Heat the oil in a pan and add ginger-garlic paste. Sauté until fragrant and add in the fried onions. Keep stirring to make sure the onions and the paste amalgamate. Pour in the lime juice and add salt. Mix well again.

Add the red chilli powder and sauté for a few more minutes to let the flavours mix well. Serve in a small bowl as an accompaniment with any meal. In our home this is always on the table.

AJAR KA ACHAAR

This is a very special recipe for me because it was my grandmother's and it tastes of my childhood.

INGREDIENTS

3 kg carrots

¼ kg sugar

200 gm salt, to soak carrots in

100 gm salt, to cook with

100 gm mustard seeds

100 gm dry chillies, ground in vinegar

1 ½ litres vinegar

1 litre oil

6 teaspoons ginger paste

3 teaspoons garlic paste

3 teaspoons ginger, finely chopped

2 teaspoons turmeric powder

METHOD

Cut the carrots into thin strips or small cubes, as you prefer. Soak these in 200 gram of salt for 3-4 hours. Wash off the salt and let the carrots dry thoroughly.

In a large vessel, heat oil. Add mustard seeds and when these splutter, toss in the carrots.

Mix well and add the pastes, ground chillies, chopped ginger, turmeric, sugar and vinegar. Keep the vessel on the stove until the carrots are cooked.

Let cool, and bottle.

Gajar Ka Achaar

HARI MIRCH ACHAAR

INGREDIENTS

½ litre vinegar

¼ litre oil

500 gm thick green chillies, washed and wiped dry

100 gm ginger

50 gm garlic

6 tablespoons sugar

1 tablespoon cumin seeds

1 tablespoon mustard seeds

1 tablespoon tamarind paste

1 teaspoon turmeric powder

1 sprig curry leaves

Salt to taste

METHOD

Cut the clean, dry chillies into ½" pieces. Rub them with a teaspoon of salt. Set aside.

Grind ginger, garlic and cumin seeds with vinegar. Heat oil and add mustard seeds. As soon as these crackle, take the pan off the stove and put in the ground masala and turmeric powder. Return to the stove and let the spices cook for a few minutes. Add in the chillies, tamarind paste, sugar and salt. Mix well, and throw in the curry leaves. Cook on slow fire for 15 minutes. Allow to cool and then store in a bottle.

SABZI KA ACHAAR

INGREDIENTS

1 kg mixed vegetables, such as carrots, small onions, radishes, peas, cauliflower florets

2 cups oil

1 cup sugar

A handful of curry leaves for the baghar

Salt to taste

Grind the following into a paste

¼ cup vinegar

20 Kashmiri chillies

2 garlic cloves

½" piece dried turmeric

4 teaspoons mustard seeds

2 teaspoons cumin seeds

1 teaspoon fenugreek seeds

METHOD

Clean all the vegetables and cut into medium-sized pieces. Sprinkle with salt and dry in the sun for a day. Discard the water that is drawn out. In a pan, heat oil until it smokes and add curry leaves and the ground masala. Fry well

Add the sugar. The flavour needs to be slightly tart but not too sharp. You may add more vinegar to achieve this. Then mix in the vegetables and cook on a slow flame for 20 minutes. Let it cool and then bottle.

Sabzi ka Achaar

BAINGAN KA ACHAAR

INGREDIENTS

1 litre vinegar

½ kg oil

750 gm eggplants

150 gm sugar

30 gm green chillies

30 gm dried red chillies, ground in vinegar

2 sprigs curry leaves

2 tablespoons salt

½ tablespoon cumin seeds

3 teaspoons ginger, chopped

2 teaspoons garlic, chopped

2 teaspoons turmeric powder

1 teaspoon mustard seeds

1 teaspoon black pepper

½ teaspoon fenugreek seeds

METHOD

Wash, dry and cube the eggplants. Soak the cubes in salted water for 3-4 hours. Grind the green and red chillies, turmeric powder, black pepper and fenugreek, mustard and cumin seeds to a fine paste, using as much vinegar as you need.

Bring the oil to a boil in a large pan. Add this ground masala and fry until fragrant. Then, add the ginger, garlic and curry leaves. Mix well. Lastly, mix in the eggplants and sugar. Add in the remaining vinegar and leave on a slow fire until the eggplants are cooked and the gravy thickens. Cool and bottle.

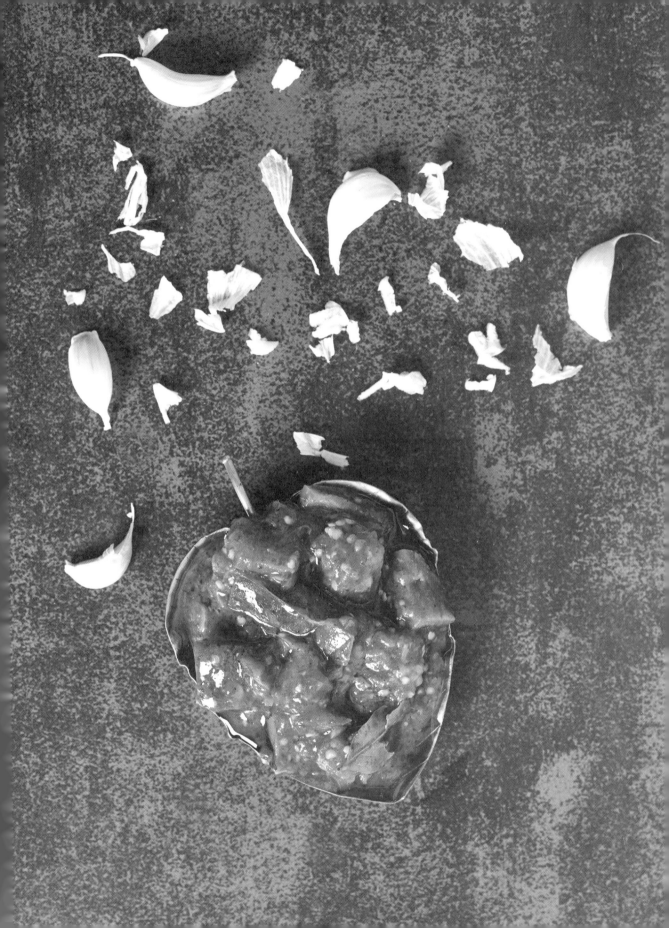

GOSHT KI CHUTNEY

You will need a good-quality mortar and pestle to get the desired consistency – it is impossible to achieve it using a blender.

INGREDIENTS

½ kg boneless mutton, with no fat

1 tablespoon unroasted coriander powder

2 teaspoons chilli powder

½ teaspoon turmeric powder

Salt to taste

Lightly roast and grind

2½ tablespoons patthar ka phool

2½ tablespoons ginger-garlic paste

1½ tablespoons peanuts

1½ tablespoons sesame seeds

1 tablespoon cumin seeds

1 tablespoon mustard seeds

¼ teaspoon fenugreek seeds

For the tadka

6 dried red chillies

3 garlic cloves

2 sprigs curry leaves

2 teaspoons cumin seeds

1 teaspoon mustard seeds

A pinch of asafoetida

METHOD

Clean the meat and cut into small cubes. Wash with salt and set aside in a plastic container.

Heat oil in a deep pan and then lower the flame, and add a pinch of cumin seeds, a few curry leaves and a garlic clove. Mix in the masala you have roasted and ground; sauté until fragrant.

Add in the meat, cover immediately and let cook in its own juices. When it softens, uncover the pan and allow the liquid to form a thick gravy.

Wash the mortar and pestle, and make sure it's clean and dry.

When the meat is cool enough to work with – but not cold – start grinding it, a cupful at a time, to a fine paste. Let this paste cool completely in a deep bowl.

To add the tadka, heat the oil in a frying pan and add all the ingredients. Allow the chillies to fry well, until nearly charred. Pour this baghar over the ground meat and cover the bowl immediately. Set aside for 2 to 3 hours to allow the flavours to combine.

Store in the refrigerator. Take each serving out just before you'd like to eat it, and warm it either on a low flame or in the microwave.

HATTA MEETHA AAM CHUTNEY

INGREDIENTS

1 kg semi-ripe mangoes

100 gm jaggery

2 tablespoons tamarind juice

1 tablespoon oil

2 teaspoons chilli powder

Salt to taste

METHOD

Peel the mangoes and cube them.

Heat oil in a pan and add the mangoes and chilli powder. Let the mixture cook for 5 minutes before adding in jaggery, tamarind juice and salt. Mix well to combine all the flavours and let the chutney come to a boil. Lower the flame and let it cook for five more minutes. Take the pan off the flame and let the chutney cool before you serve it.

HOOP NIMBU

For a pickle that takes so little effort and time to make, it's much more delicious than you might think it will be. If you store it in the fridge, it will keep for a year. Please note that you need 60 limes in total because you use the whole limes in the pickle.

INGREDIENTS

30 limes, cleaned and left whole

30 limes, to juice

20 whole green chillies

Salt to taste

METHOD

Make sure the 30 whole limes are dry, and prick holes over them.

Juice the other 30 limes.

Put the whole limes and green chillies into a jar and pour the lime juice and salt over.

Shake well and keep in the sun for at least a week. The limes should swell up and change colour. Store in the fridge.

To serve, remove one or two limes, as you need, and as many green chillies as you would like. Cut the limes into pieces and leave the chillies whole.

Allow to cool and then store in a bottle.

Khatta Meetha Aam Chutney

NDE KA ACHAAR

A delicious way to use eggs, this pickle keeps for two weeks in the fridge.

INGREDIENTS

3 cups vinegar

12 hard boiled eggs, shelled

12 cloves

12 peppercorns

6 dried red chillies

4 garlic cloves

1" cinnamon stick

1" piece ginger

1 tablespoon mustard seeds, coarsely ground

½ teaspoon sugar

Salt to taste

METHOD

Grind ginger and garlic together. In a pan, combine this paste with all the ingredients, except the eggs. Bring the mixture to the boil and let it simmer for 15 minutes. Strain it and let cool.

Put all the eggs in a large jar with a tight lid. Pour the strained vinegar into the jar, shut tight and leave it be for a week in a cool, dry place.

TAAZA JHINGA KE ACHAAR

INGREDIENTS

¼ kg prawns, cleaned and minced

250 ml tomato puree

¾ cup vinegar

3 onions, minced

3 to 4 green chillies

5 teaspoons sugar

3 teaspoons chilli powder

3 teaspoons cumin powder

3 teaspoons mustard seeds, ground

3 teaspoons ginger-garlic paste

2 teaspoons salt

1 teaspoon turmeric powder

METHOD

Wash and dry prawns. Heat oil in a pan and add salt and turmeric, mixed together. Fry for a minute or two before adding in the onions, and let these brown.

In the meantime, mix the ginger-garlic paste, ground mustard seeds and chilli and cumin powders with the vinegar. Then, add curry leaves into the pan with the masala and vinegar paste. Fry for a few minutes, and pour in the tomato puree. When all the ingredients in the pan are well amalgamated, add prawns, sugar and green chillies. Cook until the prawns are soft. Let it cool before decanting into a bottle.

Ande ka Achaar

In The City
of
Saffron and Pearls

WARP AND WEFT : Preserving History

No matter how busy my day, or how much I have on my plate, the one thing I never compromise on is paying attention to my outfit. I love textiles, traditional Indian craftsmanship and jewellery – I always have, even as a young girl, and over the years, it has truly become a passion of mine. Which is why I love visiting the headquarters of Suraiya Apa's weaving unit, which she runs out of our family farmhouse in Hyderabad, with help from Dominic, my brother-in-law.

Weavers, trained by her, spin truly magnificent bolts of Persian brocades such as mashru, himroo, jamavar and paithani,

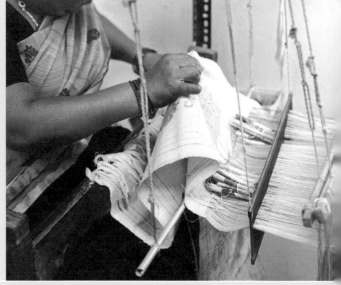

reviving ancient crafts. She also sources kalamkari, ikat and linen fabrics as well as the most beautiful and unique sarees. My weakness, I must confess, are these sarees and over the decades, I have managed to build a collection of ikats, especially in cotton and silk, that I truly treasure, and that win me countless compliments every time I wear them. Visiting the farm and spending time with Suraiya Apa is a very important part of my frequent trips home to Hyderabad. As a family, we are very grateful for the opportunity to revive these traditional crafts and provide employment to underprivileged women; there is also a school on the premises, so the children of the employees are catered to as well.

Perhaps in a different life I might have studied fashion but even without formal training, I did run a successful boutique for many years, creating Indian wear that was designed by me and embellished by very skilled craftsmen. My visits to the farm and my own collection of these priceless weaves help me maintain a deep connection with fashion, craftsmanship and textiles – which is why sharing this part of my life has been an important story in the book.

Snacks

ONE-BY-TWO PAUNA: Where Have All The Irani Cafes Gone?

*I*n Vienna and Paris, one goes to a cafe for coffee; in Shanghai and Tokyo, one goes to a teahouse for tea. Only in Hyderabad would you go to a cafe for tea. And thereby hangs a tale.

If you were a student, taxi driver, government clerk, political activist, poet or an unemployed youth in the Hyderabad of the 1960s and 1970s, chances are you would have spent long hours in an Irani cafe, seated on a bentwood chair with a round seat, with a cup of tea on the glass- or marble-topped table in front of you.

Immigrant Iranis brought the European cafe culture to Bombay first, and when they discovered that the city preferred tea to coffee, they, of course, offered it in a cafe. From Bombay, the Irani cafe made its way to Hyderabad and eventually, there was one on every street corner between the city's Hussain Sagar Lake and Charminar – Cafe Khayyam, Cosmopolitan Cafe, Azizia Cafe, Garden Cafe...the list went on. And with each cafe grew a culture rich with food and drink, its own vocabulary and a repository of stories.

'*Ek pauna, do biskoot*,' the server would shout as a customer slowly made his way out. The word

pauna derives from *pau*, which means a quarter. A quarter of the teacup is left empty so that two spoons of thick milk and two spoons of sugar can be added to dark, over-boiled tea. Dark brown, milky, sweet – the pauna came served in small teacups. The manager, seated at the door which served as both entrance and exit, would of course know precisely which customer should be charged for it. There were no bills, no frills. The server's memory was all. Try walking out without paying the bill, the server would only shout louder and more forcefully – 'Ek pauna, do biskoot!' Everyone paid.

That practice of billing you by shouting out your order generated its own humour. Those who sat long hours ordering nothing – as we did – had a self-deprecatory announcement that would declare our exit – '*Khaaya nai, peeya nai, glass thoda. Chaaranai.*' ('Ate nothing. Drank nothing. Broke a glass. Four annas!)

It was a measure of the Irani owner's indulgence towards us students that we would very often step into a cafe merely to grab chairs and sit around a table discussing student politics, the writing of Marx and Kafka, the films of Ray and

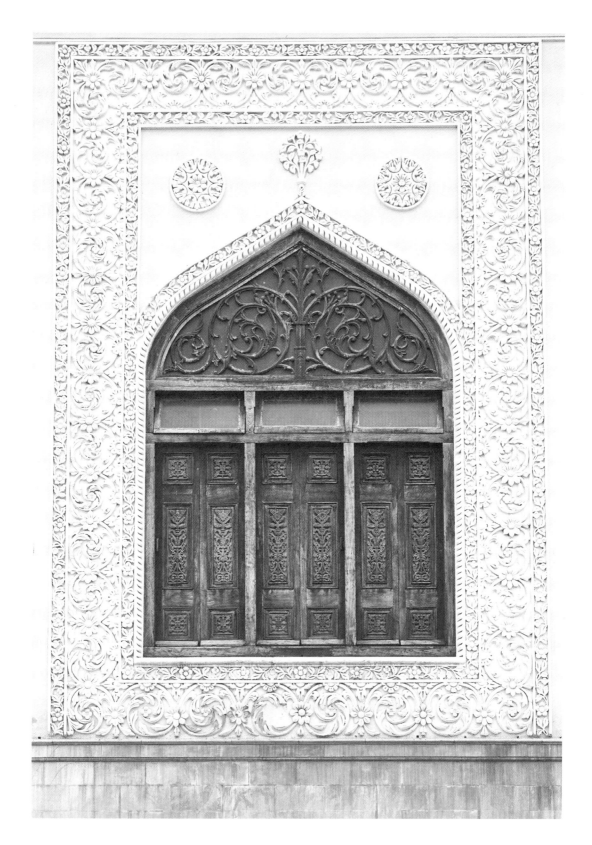

Wajda or which guy that girl was looking at. Endless cups of tea would be ordered, but often shared in a one-by-two pauna – half the tea remained in the cup, the other half was poured onto the saucer and slurped down. A metaphor of our times.

For my generation of Hyderabadi students, and indeed for that of Peter Hassan and his friends, Irani cafes were the place to hang out. There was not a day during my time in Nizam College that my friends and I would not find ourselves in one. Our tea was accompanied by the famous sweet-and-salty Osmania biscuits, which were named for the last Nizam of Hyderabad, Mir Osman Ali Khan. Baked with almost equal amounts of butter and sugar, it is that pinch of salt that gives the Osmania biscuit its edge.

A hungry taxi driver would of course want something more substantial such as bun-maska served with an omelette. My personal favourite at an Irani cafe was always the small, crispy onion samosa. Deep-fried, the thin pastry layer gives it crispness, and the combination of the onion and coriander filling is full of flavour. Some cafes offered another Hyderabadi variant of the samosa – the lukhmi. One could get a vegetable lukhmi filled with potato or a non-vegetarian version with kheema. The lukhmi's outer layer is thicker than that of an onion samosa. For a Hyderabadi in New Delhi the only place to go for a lukhmi, if one is lucky, is the home of Doreen and Peter Hassan.

Doreen and Peter have come to represent the best of Hyderabadi cuisine in New Delhi. Most imagine that Hyderabad's speciality is its dum biryani but thanks to Doreen, her guests know that our city's exquisite cuisines also includes such vegetarian dishes as Tamatar ka Kut (page 38) and Mirchi ka Saalan (page 44). On a lucky evening, you get to taste Khubooli, yet another Hyderabadi speciality (page 132).

Until 1978, every Irani cafe displayed the handsome and regal portrait of the Shah of Iran, Mohammad Reza Pahlavi. When the Shah visited Hyderabad in the early 1970s, every Irani cafe owner lined up on the tarmac at Begumpet Airport to welcome him. They kneeled to greet him, and as he and his beautiful wife, Empress Farah, walked down the red carpet, the loyal Iranians kissed the ground on which their majesties had walked. After the revolution, however, the Shah's portraits were taken down and replaced with even larger portraits of Ayatollah Khomeini. Even so, the Irani at the counter neither had an interest in politics back home nor the politics we would be discussing at his tables. He was happy swatting flies, collecting money and keeping an eye on his staff.

Today, many associate Hyderabad's cafes with biryani. In my student days, though, few cafes served food and fewer still served biryani. The Irani cafe was not a place you went to for a meal. Like European cafes, one went there for beverages and perhaps a snack. One such was a professor from Cambridge University, UK, who had been told that the best biryani in Hyderabad was to be found at an Irani cafe near Charminar, and so I took her there for lunch.

The manager at the counter was flabbergasted and remonstrated us – 'No place for zenana!' The lady was willing to sit in the general section and to find the middle path, the manager immediately summoned a screen and placed it around the table!

Doreen tells us how she and her friends would have runners called baharwalas to fetch snacks for them from a cafe because women would not be allowed in. At Cosmopolitan Cafe in Narayanaguda, however, things were different. An army of us student activists, boys and girls, would invade it and have long arguments in loud voices. The manager had to just put up with it.

In a fit of nostalgia, I decided to visit an Irani cafe on a recent visit to Hyderabad. I drove to every street corner I knew but in vain. In my familiar childhood neighbourhood of Himayatnagar, Cafe Khayyam was gone. Cosmopolitan was still there, but no longer called a cafe, and now serving only 'North Indian & Chinese'. At the Bashir Bagh crossroad, down the road from Nizam College, the cafe of our student days was no longer to be found. I drove all the way through Abids and on to Charminar, via Sultan Bazar and Jambagh, returning home through Moazamjahi Market and Nampally. None of the familiar cafes were there. In Himayatnagar, no one I spoke to knew there

was once a Morine Cafe. In what seems to be an Americanization of the culture of eating out, Irani cafes have been replaced by places that call themselves 'fast food', 'restaurant' or even 'hotel'. Not cafe. And almost every place display boards letting you know that biryani and haleem are on offer. Secunderabad's Garden Cafe now calls itself Garden Restaurant. Shah Ghouse Cafe and Nimrah Cafe & Bakery, near Charminar, were the odd ones out. Their names figure on exotic tourist websites. Neither is worth a visit, sadly.

Not surprisingly, there is a Chicago Cafe near the U.S. consulate in Begumpet. It serves authentic Irani chai and Osmania biscuits. But it also offers a south Indian meal and snacks like aloo-poori. I stepped into many of these newer places, wherever I could find parking space for my car, but I did not go back in time as I had hoped to. The lazy ambiance of the past was gone. It was 'fast food' alright. Everyone was in a hurry to order, eat, drink and go. There was no server shouting out the bill to the manager at the door. You got a piece of paper. There were no students sitting around tables and plotting revolutions. More than the change of a name, what saddened me was the change in culture. With the word 'cafe' gone, they no longer have the convivial atmosphere of one.

My nostalgia punctured, I decided to make one last halt at a famous haleem place near my house in Banjara Hills. The name – Sarvi Take-Away – was not very inspiring but I decided to stop for a chai and samosa. The former was nothing special but the latter managed to do what I had hoped for – it took me back four decades.

Dr Sanjaya Baru

NION SAMOSA

INGREDIENTS

1 cup beaten rice

1 cup onions, chopped

1 cup wheat flour

1 cup plain flour

1 bunch coriander leaves, chopped

3 green chillies, chopped

1 teaspoon chilli powder

½ teaspoon chaat masala

½ teaspoon cumin powder

Water, as required

Salt to taste

Oil

METHOD

In a bowl, add both flours, salt, a teaspoon of oil and, using a little water at a time, knead a soft dough. Cover and keep aside to rest for 10 minutes.

Add the chopped onions, coriander leaves and green chillies with poha, chilli powder, cumin powder and chat masala in another bowl. Mix well to combine.

Mix a teaspoon of plain flour with water to form a paste in a separate smaller bowl.

Take the prepared dough out of the bowl, and roll out thin circles, like rotis.

Cook each roti lightly, on both sides.

When all are done, cut each into a triangular shape.

Apply the flour paste on one side. Place the mixture of onions in the centre and seal the edges.

Heat the oil in a pan until very hot. Do not crowd the samosas as you should be able to turn each over. Deep fry until golden brown. Remove onto a large plate or platter lined with absorbent paper.

EGG PUFFS

INGREDIENTS

To make the pastry
250 gm plain flour
20 gm butter
10 gm sugar
5 gm salt
130 ml water

Juice of half a lime
To make the puff
2 boiled eggs, hard boiled
2 teaspoons oil
Black pepper powder to taste
Salt to taste

METHOD

TO MAKE THE PASTRY

To the flour, add salt, sugar, water and lemon juice. Knead well and allow the dough to rest. Refrigerate for 20 minutes, covered with a damp cloth.

Divide the butter into three equal parts. Store in a cool place but not in the fridge. You need the butter to stay soft so you can spread it.

Roll dough into a thin rectangle.

Take one part of the butter and spread it on two-thirds of the dough. Pick up the unbuttered section of the dough and fold the rectangle three times. Place on a plate, cover with a damp cloth and put it in the fridge for 15 minutes.

Take the dough out, and roll it out again into a rectangle of similar size and thinness as the last time.

Spread the second part of the butter on two-thirds of the dough. Fold as before into three, place on a plate, cover with a damp cloth and put it in the fridge for 15 minutes.

Take the dough out and roll into a rectangle, as before. Spread the last part of the butter on the whole rectangle. Fold each end towards the middle, and fold into two. Return to the fridge, covered with a damp cloth for 15 minutes.

Take the dough out and roll into a square. Cut the square into quarters.

TO MAKE THE PUFF

Take one quarter of the dough and place one egg half in the centre of the square. Sprinkle with pepper and salt to taste. Bring two of the opposite ends to the centre and seal, using a little water. The other two ends remain open.

Once all four puffs are ready, brush each one with milk or water. Bake in a preheated oven at 220° Celsius for 20 minutes.

If you have any leftover pastry, cut into thin strips and twist each in the centre, so it resembles a bow. Brush each strip with milk or water and bake along with the puffs. This is a good snack to have on hand.

PALAK PAKORA

INGREDIENTS

1 cup gram flour

12-15 medium-sized spinach leaves

1 teaspoon red chilli powder

1 teaspoon turmeric powder

¾ teaspoon carom seeds

A pinch of baking soda

A pinch of asafoetida

Water as required, to make the batter

Oil for frying

Salt to taste

Chaat masala to sprinkle on top

METHOD

Separate the spinach leaves and wash thoroughly. Lay out on clean cloth.

Mix the gram flour, asafoetida with red chilli powder, turmeric powder, carom seeds and baking soda.

Adding water a little bit at a time, create a silky-smooth batter.

Heat oil in a deep pan until very hot. Dip spinach leaves one at a time into the batter and drop into the hot oil. Fry until beautifully golden brown in colour.

Remove onto a large plate or platter lined with absorbent paper. If you like, you can sprinkle a little chaat masala on the pakoras before you serve.

IRCHI BHAJJIS

INGREDIENTS

1 cup gram flour

8 to 10 long, fat green chillies

1½ teaspoon carom seeds

½ teaspoon chilli powder

¼ teaspoon baking powder

¼ teaspoon chaat masala

¼ teaspoon baking soda

A berry-sized ball of tamarind (the size of a gooseberry)

Salt to taste

Water as required, to make the batter

Oil for frying

METHOD

Soak tamarind, ajwain seeds, salt, red chilli powder and chaat masala for 15 to 20 minutes in a bowl. Grind to a fine paste.

Wash green chillies well, allow to dry and slit lengthwise. De-seed and stuff each chilli with one teaspoon of tamarind paste.

Mix in the gram flour, salt and baking soda in a bowl. Adding a little water at a time, make a silky-smooth batter.

Pour the oil in a pan and keep checking. Allow to heat well.

Drop the chillies in but do not crowd the pan. You should be able to turn each one over. Fry each chilli until golden brown in colour.

Remove onto a large plate or platter lined with absorbent paper. Either serve each chilli whole or slice into roundels.

Sweets

URAN POORI

Many communities make a version of puran poli, but this is an extremely unusual recipe, which I learnt from our aunt, Zehra Phuppu, in my first cooking lesson. It is a bit indulgent in our health-conscious age but I recommend you try it at least once – it is absolutely delicious and you will not regret it.

INGREDIENTS

3 kg sugar

2 kg ghee

1 kg Bengal gram

1 kg semolina

½ kg almonds, blanched and ground to a fine paste

3 cardamoms, peeled and powdered

A few strands of saffron

Water as needed

METHOD

Boil the Bengal gram until it is very soft. Strain it, let it cool just a bit and then mash it to a fine paste.

In a large, heavy-bottomed pan, put half the ghee to heat. Add the mashed dal and sauté on a low flame until brown. Very carefully, drain off the remaining ghee into a bowl and set aside.

Continue cooking the paste on a low flame and add the ground almonds, saffron and sugar. Mix well to combine and let it all cook to a fine consistency. Take the pan off the flame and set aside.

Mix the semolina, remaining ghee and as much as water as you need to make a soft, pliable dough. Roll out thin rotis and cook each on both sides on a tawa.

Grease a large baking dish or lagan and arrange a layer of the rotis on the bottom. Cover with a layer of the dhal mixture and pour ghee over it.

Repeat until you have used up all the rotis, mixture and ghee. The last pour of ghee needs to be more generous than the rest.

Cover with foil and bake in a hot oven. If you are using a lagan, you can cook this over coals. Do place some hot coals on top of the dish as well. In 30 minutes, the puran poori should be golden brown in colour.

Leave it aside to cool, cut into thin slices and serve.

HIRNEE

In our early years in Delhi, after I'd mastered the biryani and could cook a spread for dinner, we still ordered in dessert. Peter liked to serve phirnee, which he would get from the Old City. It was delicious, of course, and I would often ask him if it was expensive but he always said no. And then one day, the man delivered the phirnee when I was home alone so I asked for the bill. It turned out to be ₹11 per bowl, which was a lot in those days. I decided right then and there to learn how to make phirnee.

As it happened, I'd seen a recipe for it in a magazine, but now I've forgotten which one it was. The next time Peter was out of town, I tried my hand at making phirnee and my father, who was visiting us at the time, said it was very good. He thought it was even better than what we ordered from the Old City, which boosted my confidence.

Before our next dinner party, I told Peter not to order dessert. I made the phirnee and served it in earthen bowls, arranged very prettily on a big platter decorated with rose petals. It won me many compliments and the recipe I found by chance in a magazine is now one of my favourites. It makes enough for 15 servings.

INGREDIENTS

2 litres milk
½ kg sugar
¼ kg fresh cream
¼ kg rice

10 tablespoons almonds, finely chopped
10 tablespoons pistachios, finely chopped
2 teaspoons almond essence
Varaq for garnish

METHOD

Wash and soak rice for an hour. Then grind to a very smooth paste and keep aside.

In a large, thick-bottomed pan, put the milk to boil. Once it comes to a boil, take the pan off the flame and mix in the ground rice. Return the pan to the stove and allow the milk and rice mixture to thicken, stirring continuously to ensure it stays very smooth.

Mix in sugar and fresh cream as the mixture thickens. Continue stirring and cooking for 10 more minutes. Just a minute before it is done, mix in the almond essence.

Take the pan off the flame and spoon the phirnee into bowls. Cover each with a piece of varaq and garnish with almonds and pistachios.

Store these in the refrigerator or serve at room temperature.

SHEER KHORMA

INGREDIENTS

3 litres milk

300 gm vermicelli

250 gm sugar

75 gm pistachios, soaked for 3 hours, chopped

75 gm almonds, blanched and finely chopped

50 gm raisins, finely chopped

1 tin condensed milk

15 dry dates, deseeded and sliced lengthwise

9 tablespoons ghee

A few strands of saffron

METHOD

Melt ghee, add vermicelli in a large pan. Immediately lower the flame and fry until the vermicelli turns a light golden brown. Add milk and bring to a slow boil. Then, add condensed milk, dates and raisins. Allow the mixture to thicken on a low flame.

Serve by pouring into a large, deep bowl and decorate with pistachios and almonds.

KHUBANI KA MEETHA

This is our family recipe for the quintessentially Hyderabadi dessert. Use good-quality apricots that are sweet enough for you to leave the sugar out altogether. I prefer that natural sweetness.

INGREDIENTS

1 kg apricots

75 gm almonds, blanched and finely chopped

½ teaspoon cochineal (red food colouring)

A few drops of vanilla essence

4 tablespoons sugar

METHOD

Soak apricots overnight in enough water to cover them. Deseed them the next morning. Break the seeds and remove the almonds that are tucked inside. Soak these in hot water and peel. Set aside to use as a garnish later.

Boil the apricots in enough water to cover them. Add more water later, if required. The apricots need to break down into a thick paste. Taste for sweetness and add sugar accordingly. Do not add more than four tablespoons, though. Mix in cochineal and vanilla essence and cook for a few minutes to let the sugar melt.

Take the pan off the flame and allow the apricot mixture to cool. You can either blend this to create a smooth, thick paste or keep the consistency chunky. Pour into a bowl and decorate with the almonds you had set aside earlier. Serve with fresh cream or a custard.

Sheer Khorma

OUBLE KA MEETHA

This dish is named so because bread is known as double roti in Hyderabad. It is also called Shahi Tukra.

INGREDIENTS

1 loaf sliced bread	5 cups milk
1 brick ice cream	5 cups water
50 gm cashew nuts, crumbled	5 cups sugar
50 gm raisins	1 litre oil
50 gm chironjee	A few cardamoms, roughly powdered

METHOD

Cut the bread slices into halves and set aside. Heat water and dissolve the sugar in it. Then, add milk and cardamom powder. Pour this into the serving dish.

Heat oil and fry a few bread slices at a time until golden brown. Remove onto a plate lined with absorbent paper, and set aside. When all the slices are fried, place them in the milk mixture in the serving dish. Allow them to soak up all the liquid.

Fry the chironjee, then the cashew nuts and, finally, the raisins. in the same oil Set aside. Strain the oil and set aside too. Just before you are ready to serve, whip the ice-cream (or cream) to soften it and cover the top of the Double ka Meetha with it. Sprinkle the fried toppings on it and dribble a tablespoon of the oil over.

ADAAM KE PAAN

INGREDIENTS

1 ½ cup almonds, blanched and ground to a fine paste	¾ cup sugar
	1-2 teaspoons green food colouring
1 cup water	1 teaspoon milk
1 cup cloves	Varaq to garnish

METHOD

In a large pan, mix sugar and water and cook into a thick syrup. Add milk and the almond paste and keep stirring until the mixture leaves the sides of the pan. Take off the flame and mix in as much green food colouring as you like; ideally, it should be the colour of a paan leaf. Form a soft dough using your fingers. Divide this dough into small portions. Roll out each portion and fold into the shape of a paan. Secure with a clove.

Cover with varaq and serve on a silver platter.

Badaam ke Paan

BADAAM KI JALI

INGREDIENTS

450 gm sugar

2 cups almonds

1 cup water

6 tablespoons milk

½ tablespoon cardamom powder

METHOD

Soak almonds overnight in water. The next morning, blanch them and grind to a fine paste using milk. Boil the water and 225 gram sugar to make a syrup. Flavour with cardamom powder.

Mix the almond paste into the sugar syrup. Cook over a medium flame until the mixture leaves the sides of the pan and forms a ball. Take the pan off the stove and let the paste cool slightly. Roll into lime-sized balls. Grind the rest of the sugar to a very fine powder. Dust a board with this. On this board, roll half the balls into flat 2" rounds. Place these on a greased baking tray and moisten the sides by dipping your finger into a bowl of water and tracing the sides.

Cut out pieces of varaq and cover each round with one. Roll out the rest of the almond balls into 2" rounds. Use a cutter or mould to create a design on these. Lay each one on top of the varaq-covered rounds on the baking tray. Bake in a preheated oven at 190° for 20 minutes. The rounds should not brown but they should dry out. Cool and store. To serve, place on a pretty platter and scatter with rose petals.

BADAAM KA HALWA

INGREDIENTS

200 gm almonds, ground

200 gm sugar

150 ml fresh cream

75 gm unsalted butter

To garnish

10 almonds, soaked and peeled

10 pistachios, shelled and finely sliced

METHOD

Melt the butter in a thick-bottomed pan. Just as it begins to froth, lower the heat and add ground almonds, sugar and cream. Cook on a low heat for 10 to 15 minutes.

When the mixture darkens in colour, take off the heat and pour into a flat, greased dish. Smooth the top with a spatula. Garnish with the peeled almonds and sliced pistachios.

Slice into squares and serve. You can substitute the sugar with 5 tablespoons of Diabliss, if you would prefer that. The taste does not change at all.

Badaam Ki Jali

DAHI KE LAUZ

'Lauz' is the Hyderabadi word for a peda or a barfi.

INGREDIENTS

1 litre milk

1 cup yogurt

1 cup sugar

Powdered cardamoms to garnish

A length of clean, fine muslin

METHOD

Tie the yogurt in the muslin cloth and let all liquid drain off. In a thick-bottomed pan, boil milk until it reduces to half. Take off the stove and let cool. Mix in the drained yogurt and sugar, and pass the mixture through a strainer. The consistency needs to be very smooth. Spoon the smooth milk and yogurt mix into a baking dish, and place it in a water bath.

Place this water bath over a low flame and cook until the mixture sets. Do not cover the water bath, and make sure that the water does not dry up. So, keep hot water at hand to refill, if needed. When the milk and yogurt mixture sets, take the water bath off the flame. Cut into squares and garnish with powdered cardamom; it can be stored in an airtight container in a cool place. Serve in a flat silver dish.

ANDE KE LAUZ

INGREDIENTS

½ kg sugar

½ kg ghee

½ kg khoya

12 eggs

4 cardamoms, powdered

A few raisins, shredded

A few almonds, shredded

A few strands of saffron, melted in a little water

A little grated nutmeg

METHOD

Beat eggs, sugar, khoya and ghee together. Mix in shredded almond and raisins. Heat ghee in a pan and cook this mixture over a low flame, stirring all the time to prevent burning or curdling. When the mixture starts leaving the sides of the pan, take it off the flame and add melted saffron, nutmeg and cardamom powder.

Pour into a greased dish and bake in an oven at 150° Celsius until the top is light brown.

Let it cool, cut into diamond-shaped pieces and serve.

Ande Ke Lauz

OWRIS

This is a Hyderabadi dessert, which is like a Goan one called Neori. I love this sweet very much, though I don't make it very often.

INGREDIENTS

For the pastry
½ kg plain flour, or maida
1 cup ghee
A pinch of salt
Water to knead the dough
For the filling
½ kg semolina

½ kg sugar
¼ cup ghee
1 coconut, grated
3 tablespoons cashew nuts
½ teaspoon cardamom powder
Cornflour for dusting

METHOD

TO MAKE THE PASTRY

Mix the ghee and flour, using your fingers, until the mixture resembles fine breadcrumbs.

Dissolve the salt in the water. Use this to make a pliable dough. Cover and set aside in a cool place.

TO MAKE THE FILLING

Heat the ghee in a pan until it starts bubbling. Add in the semolina and fry well, stirring from time to time so that it is evenly and lightly browned.

Add sugar and turn the heat down. Stir continuously until the mixture dries up. Add grated coconut and cook for a while more.

Add cashew nuts, raisins and cardamom powder. Mix well to combine.

Take the pan off the flame and let the filling cool.

TO MAKE THE PATTIES

Apply ghee on nine chapattis and dust with cornflour. Layer them, with the greased side facing up. The last layer needs to be an ungreased chapatti.

Roll out so that the layers stick to one another. Cut into rounds.

Put a spoonful of the semolina mixture in each round. Wet the edges and fold into half. With the end of a fork, scallop the edges.

Deep fry until light browned, store in an airtight jar. It will keep for at least a month.

You can skip making the nine-layer dough, if you like. Just fill each chapatti separately and fry it.

At Home with the Hassans

A HAPPY LIFE IN A HAPPY HOME

$\mathcal{G}$rowing up, my brothers and I never had rooms of our own. Ours was an open house, with family members and friends always staying over. My mother's parents lived with us and my father's mother visited often, so we slept on mattresses spread on the floor of our parents' or grandparents' bedroom. It never felt like an imposition because we didn't know any other life and ours was a very happy one.

Mummy truly is the backbone of our family, and even as adults, all three of us remain very close to her. The house comes alive when she is up and about every morning – all the grandchildren stream into her room, her sons and daughters-in-law count on her to help them out, and if I am in Delhi, I am nearly always by her side. My daughter, Rhea, who studies in Delhi lives with my family. All of this as she plans menus, supervises the cooks and gets the house in order for the inevitable party that evening.

Even before she had staff to help her as she does now, Mummy managed everything with great cheer. My father worked long hours and was often travelling, but no matter how early he left the house each morning or how late he returned at night, he would always give us hugs and kisses, even if we were asleep. My mother raised us, ran the house and cooked these huge feasts nearly every day, so it was part of our routine too.

Nihal, Sahil and I would come home from school and go straight to the kitchen. I would help my mother, while the boys hung around to chat. I don't think any of us ever went out with friends or had plans of our own – we were always together, usually in the kitchen, preparing for a dinner party! That's how we were brought up, so it is an indelible part of our lives but I do

wonder, even today, how my mother managed to make it such a seamless part of her life given that she grew up in a home that was very regimented, very quiet and completely different from the one she entered as a young bride. She had to learn how to cook, and then to host parties that might have intimidated even a professional chef.

You never knew how many people would be coming to dinner and which of them might be a celebrity, a politician, a head of state or a famous musician or sports-person. If my father said thirty people, it almost always meant fifty, and this is still true. With very little help in the kitchen, Mummy would make her signature dishes calmly, laughing and talking with the three of us and any other family members who were around. I usually helped set the table, fill the house with flowers and candles or diyas. We used

to host a legendary Christmas lunch for nearly 200 people, for which Mummy and I would cook for a day and a half while also getting the house ready for so many guests, making sure we had enough plates and cutlery, etc. And whether it was five people coming to dinner or 200, Mummy would insist on looking her best and greeting each guest with a genuine smile. I think, speaking for myself, it has been the biggest lesson I have learnt from her.

At our home, every single family member is a part of every single party. Whether we had examinations or we didn't feel like it, there was no excuse. I was in Class 12, it was the night before my final examinations and we had people over; my father insisted I come downstairs and say hello. It's still how things are at my parents' home – everyone is expected to be at a party. And there is no fawning allowed. Even if a world-famous cricketer was at our table, eating biryani, we were not encouraged to take pictures with

him or ask him for his autograph! My father has always maintained that when someone steps into our home, they are a friend, and so they must feel that this is a safe space to be themselves in.

We were never told to score high marks, and our parents never lectured us about exams. We were expected to study and do our best, of course. If one of us woke up feeling too tired to go to school, it was not seen as the end of the world. Instead, they would say, 'Okay, darling, go back to sleep.' Occasionally a teacher would summon my mother to school to complain about one of us and it was never pleasant, but when she would tell my father about it, he would say, 'Don't worry. They will all do well in life.'

Looking back now, we realize the value of what they taught us – to hold our own in a group of people, to be able to have interesting conversations about a range of topics, and to understand the value of maintaining relationships.

Anisha

MY ADVICE FOR HOSTING PARTIES

Many years ago, I had a rare free day — Peter had not made his usual call to let me know how many people were coming home for dinner – and I decided to visit an exhibition to do some shopping. When I got there, Peter called and said he had just invited twenty or thirty people over; because he knew I was out, he had sent someone to buy the meat and bring it home for me to cook. I suppose I could have got irritated but it was what it was. So, I quickly wrapped up my shopping and rushed home to make biryani for our guests. And this is the story of my life, which has been repeated countless times.

I wish I had a magic formula to give people when they ask me how I manage to cook for large parties, and host them without having a breakdown, but I don't. It has been over four decades now and has thus become second nature to me. I promise you that I have learnt by trial and error. It helps that I am not someone who loses my composure under pressure, and that I do enjoy cooking for people and welcoming them into our home. To me, there's very little difference between cooking for four people and cooking for forty because the intention is the same – to make sure that each person feels welcome, eats a delicious meal and leaves our home happy.

Hosting people is such an integral aspect of our life and home, and the whole family is involved. As Anisha has written, she and her brothers were always a part of planning and hosting, even when they were little. Today, our grandchildren are encouraged to come say hello to the guests and the little ones love toasting people with their glasses of juice, which never fails to delight everyone. Anisha always helped me in the kitchen and if she is visiting Delhi, will still do it; my sons handle the bar and the décor, with help from my daughters-in-law. We all bounce ideas off one another and together, get everything done. We've never hired caterers, or ordered food in, as a matter of principle. There's always a home-cooked meal on the table.

The most important piece of advice that I can share about hosting a party is to make it easy for yourself by being organized, playing to your strengths and keeping it simple. For example, in our home, the food we serve is primarily Hyderabadi and the dish that I am best known for is biryani. I have lost count of how many kilograms of biryani I have cooked over these decades, and boxes of it have been carted across the world on request from friends and family. I started out serving Hyderabadi food simply because it's what I learnt to cook and I found that everyone enjoyed it very much. Over the years, I've tried and perfected heirloom recipes and experimented enough to create my own, so I don't deviate from my repertoire. I also enjoy serving Goan dishes, though the lack of good seafood in Delhi does not allow for it often.

By now, I could possibly draw up a menu if I was asked to in my sleep, but it took me a while to make the right combinations. (I have offered a list of my trusted menus at the end of this chapter, to get you started.) I prefer serving time-honoured pairings such as Mirchi ka Saalan with a biryani, and Tamatar ka Kut with Khubooli, for example, to form the heart of the meal, and then I choose dishes that complement them, even if they are not always traditionally paired together. There is always enough vegetarian food on the table because I would never want a guest to go home hungry and, I need to eat too at the end of the evening!

As someone who used to cook all the meals herself, I very much appreciate the help I have now in the kitchen from my trusted cooks and staff. That said, what has not changed is that I am very involved in the making of the meal. The most important thing to do is to prepare ahead of time. Decide on your menu a day or two in advance at least. It will give you enough time to shop for what you need. Check to see what can be prepared ahead of time – you can roast or grind masalas and store them and chop vegetables too. If the recipe requires it, you must marinate the meat well in advance. Make sure you don't choose to serve too many dishes that need frying or grilling at the last minute, which might need you to be in the kitchen instead of being with your guests.

Now that I have staff members to help me, I make sure I let them know what to do so

I don't have to worry about things but I do pop into the kitchen before we serve dinner, just to make sure everything is on schedule, and there are no mishaps. Earlier, I would do everything myself, with help from Anisha and maybe one more person, but we would make sure there was a system in place and we worked as per it. For instance, I always serve dinner at 10 p.m. sharp, unless there is a compelling reason to delay it.

If something does go wrong, please don't have a meltdown. Just smile and get through the evening – if you don't tell anyone that there's been a disaster, no one will know but learn from your mistakes. At a couple of our Christmas lunches many years ago, I had a dosa station set up in the garden – we lived in Hauz Khas and our home had a lovely outdoor space. While everyone enjoyed eating hot, crisp dosas in the winter, it was difficult to organize and manage. We used to invite nearly 200 people, which meant there was a rush at the counter all afternoon. Things got chaotic and I abandoned the idea after trying it out a couple of times.

And then there have been other moments, which my children love to recall. A favourite anecdote of theirs is one about a guest who came quite late to a dinner; everyone else had eaten by then, and moved on to dessert. The children, who were quite young at the time, were eating at the table, when he went to serve himself biryani. Next to it were a bowl of raita and a bowl of ice-cream, which had melted by then. He ended up helping himself to a generous portion of ice-cream, and the kids did nothing to stop him because they wanted to see what would happen. He praised me endlessly for serving such a sweet raita with the spicy biryani, and went back for a second helping. Of course, my children thought it was priceless and they still laugh about it.

When it comes to décor, we like using fresh flowers and candles to dress the house up but never do anything too dramatic because it is our home and not a hotel. In the summer, we scatter fresh jasmine flowers on the dining table and fill bowls of water with them, which we place around the room. Sometimes, I like to combine jasmine with rose petals, which creates a beautiful blend of fragrances and the colours are quite striking. The possibilities of decorating with flowers are endless and you cannot go wrong – bunches of chrysanthemums in mason jars or diyas and lotuses floating in urlis or just simple combinations of seasonal local flowers placed in a large vase on the centre table. In the winter, I rely on candles, which I like to place in unusual jars, or bunch together on large platters. They add warmth and bring a calming energy to the room.

Don't do anything that will stress you out. If you have fun at your own party, your guests will too. That's a cardinal rule. I like getting things done well in time to catch my breath, get dressed and greet the guests as they come into our home. Before Anisha got married and moved away, she and I had a lot of fun planning our outfits and doing one another's nails after we finished cooking and before the guests started streaming in. No matter how busy my day has been and even if it is my fourth dinner in a week, I like spending time choosing what to wear and getting into the right frame of mind for the evening. No-one likes being greeted by tired hosts, and it is your responsibility to set the tone for the party.

Peter and I spend time on guest lists because it is essential to invite the right mix of people, and to make sure that no-one will feel out of place. Some evenings, our guests are a combination of business magnates, politicians, ministers, bureaucrats and journalists and some evenings, it's a small group of close friends. If we are inviting someone for the first time, we do our best to ensure that they will have some like-minded company. I like to pay attention to notice if a guest appreciated a certain dish and try to make sure a dish they enjoyed in the past is on the menu.

I have made so many wonderful friends, and had countless interesting conversations with people over the years – I would have missed out on so much if I had been annoyed or distracted. At the end of the day, I think the secret to being a good host or hostess is to plan the kind of party that you would like to go to. And don't do anything that makes you uncomfortable. People always tell us that whether it was their first time at our home or they have been coming over for decades, they feel like a part of our family. I always feel very happy whenever I hear it because I know that if that's how they feel, we've played our part well.

ONE

NARGISI KABABS
DUM KA MURGH
HALEEM
MIRCHI KA SAALAN
DAHI KI KADHI
TAMATAR KA KUT
DUM KI MACHLI
KACHCHI BIRYANI
PHIRNEE

TWO

DUM KA KHEEMA
MURGH MUSSALAM
GOSHT KI KADHI
DAHI KI KADHI
BAGHARE BAINGAN
TAMATAR KA KUT
TAMATAR KI CHUTNEY
SAFED CHAWAL
KHUBOOLI
MUTTON PULAO
DOUBLE KA MEETHA

MY FAVOURITE MENUS

THREE

TALA HUA GOSHT
KALEJI GURDA
DUM KI MACHLI
MURGH METHI
MIRCHI KA SAALAN
TAMATAR ALOO
KADDU KA DALCHA
SAFED CHAWAL

FOUR

MUTTON CHAAP
IMLI MURGH
MACHLI MAHI QALIYA
TAMATAR JHINGA
KADDU KA DALCHA
NARANGI DHAL
NIMBU ZAFRANI PULAO

THE WHITE MENU

This is one of my favourite menus, and I was inspired to create it when I heard this story. Before I recount it, however, you should know that there were two classic ways of table-setting in traditional Hyderabadi homes. Prior to the 1950s, the most popular one was the dastarkhan; a tablecloth was spread on the carpeted floor, and dishes were arranged on the cloth. Diners sat cross-legged too, and ate with their plates on the cloth.

In the early 1950s, the Paigah nobles, an aristocratic family in Hyderabad, found the dastarkhan too cumbersome. They wanted to eat dinner, especially, outdoors, dressed in flowing robes and they created the chowki form of service and dining. They would spread carpets outdoors, and cover them with white cloths called channis. Four tables, called chowkis, were placed on each carpet and covered in white tablecloths, offset by runners in red or a similarly contrasting colour. Coloured grains of rice, silver powder and rose petals were scattered around each chowki, which was set for eight people. And the meal was served.

The story that enchanted me was of a certain nawab – unfortunately, I don't know his name – who loved to serve chowki dinners on full moon nights. All the dishes served, from the khormas to pulaos to desserts, were white in colour. And the chowkis would be decorated with white jasmine flowers. Guests ate off silver plates, and the dishes were also served in silverware. My White Menu has been inspired by this anonymous nawab and his unique aesthetic. I serve this dinner on silverware too, and use white seasonal flowers in the décor.

MUTTON ISTEW

RAAN KA SAALAN

MURGHH KA SAFED PULAO

SHAHI MURGH

SAFED KHORMA

PYAZ PATHA AUR JHINGA

SAFED MIRCHI KA SAALAN

MAASH KI DHAL

RESHMI PARATHA

PHIRNEE

BADAAM KA HALWA

It's rare that one hears of an idea for a piece of work and thinks how perfectly it fits the person who's creating it. But in the case of Doreen Aunty and this book of stories and recipes, this is exactly what I feel. For over fifteen years, I've been going to dinners at her home, and the company, hospitality and food have always been exquisite. I was introduced to the treasures of Hyderabadi food through evenings at her home and have been known to be shameless when piling my plate! But beyond that, Doreen Aunty has always been able to create a certain atmosphere. I was very young – still a teenager – when she, Peter Uncle and my parents became friends. At their home, I could partake in wonderful conversations with interesting people from around the world, and find my feet in a safe and stimulating adult environment. I was always made to feel at home. I have a great love for both Doreen Aunty and Peter Uncle, and I can't wait to have this book on my shelf in my own home!

Anoushka Shankar

When I think of Hyderabad, I think of food, when I think of food, I think of Peter and Doreen Hassan's dastarkhan. Because Doreen's dastarkhan is not just about the food. It is about the warmth and grace of how it is presented and served. In this case it is both in equal measure. Difficult to draw a line. It is not just about menus and recipes but about relationships and traditions which later turn to memories and nostalgia.

Hyderabadi cuisine in the hands of Doreen comes alive. Her biryanis and pulaos retain the freshness of a breath which has acquired almost an ethereal feel. And even those who claim to have given up desserts are seen digging into her Badaam ki Jali and Khubani ka Meetha. Meera, my wife, for one.

Food is a blessing which is given as a host and received as guest. And you can feel this sacred exchange invariably happen at Doreen's table.

Muzaffar Ali

Peter and Doreen have been wonderful friends to me and my family; we first met two decades ago in Washington. We thank God for giving us their friendship, which is richly remembered for so many things, including their stories of life in India. Over the years, we have appreciated their good nature and their many acts of kindness.

H.E. Mr S.R. Nathan
(President of Singapore 1999-2011)

As a foreign envoy to India, I learnt with a seasoned and highly respected Russian colleague that India is the land of *karma bhoomi* (work), *gyana* (pure knowledge) and *prem–maitri* (love and friendship). These fundamentals of the Indian way of life came alive for Guadalupe, my wife, and me on our very first day of work in India during a lovely family dinner at Doreen and Peter's house. The sole fact of receiving an invitation for an exclusive gathering at an Indian residence at the very beginning of our tenure seemed to us quite extraordinary. Love and friendship came along with an outstanding Hyderabadi biryani, where we could savour the mix of the right amount of many ingredients. It was not a simple bouquet of senses, it was a whole spice market turned into a work of art. Khubani ka Meetha for dessert just added a sense of ethereal gustative pleasure that only Doreen's hard work and talent could have produced.

We then understood that India is the land of spices (masala bhoomi), but it takes a master to orchestrate the various flavours into something that translates into a beautiful music. Doreen is capable of that with charm and grace and a great degree of humbleness. One problem remains, however: how can one taste such good Indian cuisine outside Doreen's home? Maybe her recipes could help. Just maybe.

Guadalupe & H.E. Tovar da Silva Nunes
Ambassador of Brazil in India

Few cuisines have impressed me as much as the Hyderabadi, for its uniqueness, creativity, taste, spices, aroma and variety. And I have had the pleasure of enjoying Hyderabadi cuisine largely due to the warmth, affection and hospitality of Doreen Hassan. This book, which is a lucid, open-hearted, first-person account accompanied by brilliant photographs, is a must-read.

Amitabh Kant

Peter bhai and Doreen love having people over and when someone is genuinely joyful about your presence in their home, it shows. It shows in the smiling eyes as stories and conversations abound, and especially in the loving care with which Doreen prepares her splendid food in a home that exudes so much love and warmth.

Anita Dongre

There is a small percentage of people who look beyond their defined area and see opportunities beyond the ordinary. Doreen and Peter Hassan are two such individuals. Beyond their business and family they have reached out from New Delhi to people from many parts of the world and have made and maintained lasting friendships. It is therefore a great delight to add from New Zealand from my wife Susan and I, very best wishes on the publication of this book, in which some of this special chemistry will doubtless be exhibited.

Rt. Hon. Sir Anand Stayanand & Lady Susan
Governor General of New Zealand 2006–11

I call Doreen's house 'home', because of which I have been blessed with love, care and great soirées around the table. In the Hassan home, everything is cared for: from the way they invite you over, to how they receive you, the drinks they share with you and, most of all the food they so lavishly present to you. Love enters through the eyes and presentation and beauty is the first thing you'll remember about a meal in that household, not to mention the aromas – inviting, wholesome and warm.

H.E. Melba Pria
Ambassador of Mexico in India

We've always enjoyed the exquisite cuisine at Doreen's table. It was only earlier this year that she cooked in our kitchen in London and I was amazed at how she keeps it simple and produces the most exquisite flavours. We wish her every success with the book that she's put together with so much love.

Girija & H.E. Yash Sinha
High Commissioner of India to the United Kingdom

At Doreen and Peter's Delhi home, the delectable Hyderabadi cuisine served with generous Hyderabadi warmth is always the greatest attraction and this combination makes the table at their home among the finest in the city.

C. Raja Mohan

Doreen and Peter Hassan are known for their hospitality and the lavish and delicious spread of Hyderabadi dishes served at their well-attended parties. Having been to several banquets in their warm home, I also know that our smiling and lovely hostess is always the master chef of each superb meal. This delightful book offers those traditional recipes to everyone.

Begum Bilkis I. Latif

Doreen Hassan is the perfect hostess who believes that every occasion is a celebration and unique. As simple as she is, so are her recipes and her food introduces the rich and traditional cuisine of Hyderabad to the entire world.

Drs Radha & Raja Reddy

Doreen is legendary for her table and evenings at Peter and Doreen's are always a pleasure! Apart from the interesting conversations, it is Doreen's table laden with delicacies and treasured family recipes that are a highlight.

Priya Paul

At the risk of being stoned by Patthar ka Gosht, I am convinced that the best Hyderabadi food is not available in Hyderabad. It is in New Delhi in Doreen Hassan's home. I can vouch for this as a fairly regular visitor to her place for the last thirty-five years. Given the authentic, high quality of Hyderabadi food that she has been dishing out for more than three decades in Delhi, Doreen's book promises to be the last word in cuisine from that part of India.

Sona & Ashok Jha

This is the story of a young Goan girl who barely knew how to brew a cup of tea when she got married to a man from Hyderabad and who has transformed herself into a connoisseur of the most delicate and flavourful Hyderabadi cuisine. The thing about the Hassans, as I've seen first-hand over the years, is that the fine line between intimacy and otherness is bridged by Doreen's food.

Jyoti Malhotra

I feel very proud to say that I have always shared a very special relationship with Peter Toghrille Hassan. In my mind, the Hassan family symbolizes the unique cradle of cosmopolitan culture which was the hallmark of the Hyderabad of yesteryears. I have known many distinguished members of his family for nearly eight decades, or to be precise, since 1940.

I have known Peter, as also Doreen, on very intimate terms from their childhood days. Both of them hail from well-known Hyderabadi families. In their marriage, one saw the coming together of two of Hyderabad's prominent, highly erudite families of that memorable era, which remains etched in one's mind as a golden epoch in the annals of the state.

Nawab Shah Alam Khan

My husband's ties with the Hassans go back many years, and we have long been friends with Peter and Doreen - our children have grown up together. I love seeing her, eating the delicious meals she makes and spending time with her. Doreen's food is really the best of Hyderabadi cuisine.

Leela Khan

Dining at the Hassans' is always an unalloyed pleasure. The Hassan home is always an open house where even an impromptu meal is no less than an elaborate feast. Doreen's delectable food is doubtlessly the centrepiece of the famed Hassan hospitality. But equally exceptional is the warmth and spontaneity with which they indulge their guests, making each one feel special and wanted.

Ameeta & Rajiv Kapoor

The Hassans' hospitality is legendary and the food is to die for. I always feel so welcome the minute I step into their beautiful home. May the contents of this book inspire all everyone – be it by honing their cooking skills or just understanding the true meaning behind the saying 'united we stand, divided we fall'.

Aruna De Souza

Peter and Doreen moved from Hyderabad to Delhi where with their own brand of charm and hospitality, they quickly became the toast of the town. Whether it is in Hyderabad, Delhi, or Goa, the doors of this gracious couple's home are always thrown wide open in a warm welcome to family and friends. It is my privilege and honor to be so closely associated with the Hassans and their children.

Joyce & Felix Campos

Striking a beautiful balance of elegance, style, graciousness and warmth, Doreen and Peter have generously hosted and welcomed the world into their home on many an occasion, always turning an evening into a beautiful and memorable occasion with Peter's charisma and engaging wit and Doreen's charming and bountiful hospitality. A meal at the Hassan home is indeed a culinary and a cultural privilege.

Cleta & Rommel Valles

As aristocrats from Hyderabad, and the city from which the Nizam once ruled, Doreen and her family epitomize grace and warmth. She has an extraordinary passion for cooking in the authentic Nizami way and this book is like no other, just like the author.

Rosalita Lawrence

Doreen Fernes Hassan, with her collection of life experiences and her devotion to home and husband's personal and professional considerations, has evolved into a culinary expert in her own right, a gracious hostess and it is always a pleasure to spend time and dine with the Hassans at their homes in Delhi or in Hyderabad.

Marie & Eugene Campos

CLOSING NOTE

All her life, our mother has done everything she can to make sure that every single member of the family has achieved their dreams, and felt supported and loved. And this book has been her dream for as long as we can remember. For years – maybe even decades – Mummy has been writing down her recipes, organizing them and filing them away so when the time came to write the book, she would have everything she needed. At the same time, she has taken the care with characteristic graciousness to always remember the people who taught her how to cook each dish, when they did and why she chose to learn it.

This book is really a record of our mother's wonderful life, filled as it is with people she loves and who love her, stories of family and friends, and of course, the food that she has cooked, nearly every day for four decades, bringing all of us together to the table with generosity and happiness. As the three of us, our father, our spouses and children have been a part of the making of this book over the past year, it has given our family a chance to revisit our memories and map the journey of our family – a rare and wonderful opportunity that has reaffirmed what we have always believed. That when cooked with love and shared with a full heart, food can create abiding, precious relationships that stand the test of time.

With this collection of recipes, stories and photographs, what Mummy has done is pay homage to our families, friends and a way of life that we hope we will always honour. It contains the lessons that we have learnt from her – to pay attention to detail; to make our surroundings beautiful; to welcome people into our homes and lives with genuine hospitality; to cherish friendships and nurture them over the years; to respect every person's contribution to our lives; and to live with integrity and kindness.

Saffron and Pearls is truly Doreen Hassan's labour of love and we could not be happier or prouder of our mother.

Anisha, Nihal and Sahil

Anisha and Vijay, with Rhea and Raoul

Nihal and Neha, with Anahi and Riaan

ACKNOWLEDGEMENTS

My parents, Lui and Emma Fernes; my in-laws, Khurshid (Kuchu) and Mary Hassan; and our mentor, Abid Bhai (Abid Hussain) – though they are no longer with us, their love and support, and our family's memories of them are woven through this book.

A special thank you – Jose; Timo; Johnny; Ann; Chintara, Munna; Sumbul

In fond memory of President H. E. SR Nathan (President of Singapore 1999-2011); Bilkis Aapa (Begum Bilkis Latif); Nawab Shah Alam Khan

For their wonderful pieces and their long-standing friendships with our family –

Habib Bhai (Habib Rehman); Sunil and Marshneil Gavaskar; Sanjaya and Rama Baru; Anoushka Shankar and her dear parents, Sukanyaji and the late Pandit Ravi Shankarji.

For generously making the time to contribute – Amitabh Kant; Rt. Hon. Sir Anand Satyanand (Governor General of New Zealand, 2006-11) and Lady Susan; Anita Dongre; Aruna D'Souza; Cleta and Rommel Valles; Girija and H.E. Yashvardhan Sinha; Guadalupe and H. E. Tovar Da Silva; Joyce and Felix Campos; Jyoti Malhotra; Marie and Eugene Campos; Muzzafar Ali; H.E. Melba Pria; C. Raja Mohan; Priya Paul; Dr(s) Radha and Raja Reddy; Rajeev Kapoor; Raylin Valles; Rosalita Lawrence; Sangita and Vijay Chahal; Kitty (Sona) and Ashok Jha.

For sharing their memories and stories, which helped me put my own together – Bizeth Banerjee; Fatima Aapa (Fatima Attari); Karki Bhabi (Karki Hussain); Leela Aapa (Leela Khan); Sanjar Bhai (Sanjar Ali Khan); Suraiya Aapa (Suraiya Hassan Bose); S. Kulandaveil (Velu).

Chinmayee Manjunath, my editor, who helped me put this book together and anchored the process; and Cyrus Dalal, who helmed all the shoots – I sincerely thank them both for being such an integral a part of this journey.

At HarperCollins India, I would like to thank Shreya Punj and Ananth Padmanabhan for championing the book, and Bonita Vaz-Shimray and Natasha Chandhok for designing it.

For being a part of the team on shoots – Akshita Phoolka and Namrata Phoolka, who helped style the food; Rolika Prakash and Arvind Kumar for make-up and hair.

It would be impossible for me to name every well-wisher of mine whose unstinted support I have received over the years, as I prepared to write this book. There have been many associates, friends, family members and acquaintances who have played a part in this journey – I thank each of them with all my heart.

And finally, my love and gratitude to my husband, children and grandchildren, to whom this book is dedicated.

Doreen Hassan

Sahil and Neha, with Anaia and Aliana